# The Debate of King Milinda

# BUDDHIST TRADITION SERIES

Edited by
ALEX WAYMAN



**VOLUME 14**

# THE DEBATE OF KING MILINDA

an Abridgement of
The Milinda Pañha

Edited by
BHIKKHU PESALA

MOTILAL BANARSIDASS PUBLISHERS
PRIVATE LIMITED • DELHI

*First Edition: Delhi, 1991*
*Revised Edition: Delhi, 1998*



ISBN: 81-208-0893-2

*Also available at:*

**MOTILAL BANARSIDASS**

41 U.A. Bungalow Road, Jawahar Nagar, Delhi 110 007
8, Mahalaxmi Chamber, Warden Road, Mumbai 400 026
120 Royapettah High Road, Mylapore, Chennai 600 004
Sanas Plaza, Subhash Nagar, Pune 411 002
16 St. Mark's Road, Bangalore 560 001
8 Camac Street, Calcutta 700 017
Ashok Rajpath, Patna 800 004
Chowk, Varanasi 221 001

PRINTED IN INDIA
BY JAINENDRA PRAKASH JAIN AT SHRI JAINENDRA PRESS,
A-45 NARAINA, PHASE I, NEW DELHI 110 028
AND PUBLISHED BY NARENDRA PRAKASH JAIN FOR
MOTILAL BANARSIDASS PUBLISHERS PRIVATE LIMITED,
BUNGALOW ROAD, DELHI 110 007

## Foreword by Series Editor

*The Debate of King Milinda* as here abridged by Bhikkhu Pesala is a careful presentation of the main discourse throughout this remarkable piece of Buddhist literature. The T.W. Rhys Davids' translation of the work in its full extent is still available in volumes XXXV and XXXVI of the *Sacred Books of the East*. Granted that sometimes this old translation (published in 1890 and 1894 volumes) — although very intelligently made — is wanting here and there in how to render the Buddhist technical terms. Besides that full translation did not include a list of Pali terms, as does the Bhikkhu's present work. This abridgement should be welcomed as a sensitive up-to-date embrace of this great Buddhist classic, whose exposition of the basic Buddhist issues is perennially important. The editor takes pleasure in the inclusion of this work in the Buddhist Tradition Series.

New York City
May 24, 1990

Alex Wayman

# Foreword

by

Ven. Dr. Hammalawa Saddhātissa

The *Milinda Pañha* is a Pali book written in about the 1st century B.C. King Milinda, a Bactrian king who ruled the northeast of India, met a learned monk called Nāgasena and the king put a number of questions on the philosophy, psychology and ethics of Buddhism. I presume this debate was conducted in the Bactrian Greek language but was later translated into Pali and Sanskrit.

This well-known Pali book called *Milinda Pañha* or *Questions of King Milinda* has twice been translated into English: in 1890, and in 1969. Both translations are literary and, in many places literal, therefore they were mainly confined to scholars. This present work is, however, not a literal but a free rendering making an abridgement and aimed at the reader who prefers to take a short cut rather than the long way, notwithstanding that the latter may be very beautiful.

The framework remains the same as the original, but in many cases the number of similes used to make a point has been reduced.

The author, Bhikkhu Pesala, is a Buddhist monk who had training in Burma and Thailand whose knowledge of Pali has enabled him to check areas of ambiguous translation to compile this concise and readable work in elegant, modern English while his knowledge of Buddhism has enabled him to clarify some obscure ideas.

This book will certainly serve its intended aim by the uncomplicated presentation of the original work.

# CONTENTS

# Abbreviations

| | Pali text | English Translation |
|---|---|---|
| A. | Aṅguttara Nikāya | Gradual Sayings |
| *A. | | Commentary on * |
| Ap. | Apadāna | |
| Asl. | Atthasālinī | The Expositor |
| B.D. | | The Book of the Discipline |
| Budv. | Buddhavaṃsa | Chronicle of the Buddhas |
| Cp. | Cariyāpiṭaka | Basket of conduct |
| D. | Dīgha Nikāya | Dialogues of the Buddha |
| Dhp. | Dhammapada | Dhammapada |
| Dhs. | Dhammasaṅgani | Buddhist Psychological Ethics |
| Dial. | | Dialogues of the Buddha |
| DPPN | | Dictionary of Pali Proper Names |
| GS. | | Gradual Sayings |
| Iti. | Itivuttaka | Manual of a Mystic |
| Ja. | Jātaka | Jātaka |
| KS. | | Kindred Sayings |
| Ku | Khuddaka Nikāya | |
| Kvu. | Kathāvatthu | Points of Controversy |
| M. | Majjhima Nikāya | Middle Length Sayings |
| Mhvs. | Mahāvaṃsa | Chronicle of Ceylon |
| Miln. | Milinda Pañha | Questions of King Milinda (R.D.)<br>Milinda's Questions (Horner) |
| MilnṬ. | Milinda Ṭika | |
| MLS. | | Middle Length Sayings |
| MQ. | | Milinda's Questions |
| PED. | | Pali-English Dictionary |
| Ppn. | | Path of Purification |
| PTS. | | Pali Text Society |
| Pṭs. | Paṭisambhidāmagga | Path of Discrimination |
| Pts.Contr. | | Points of Controversy |
| Pug. | Puggalapaññatti | Designation of Human Types |
| QKM. | | Questions of King Milinda |
| S. | Saṃyutta Nikāya | Kindred Sayings |
| Sn. | Sutta Nipāta | The Group of Discourses |
| Sta. | Sutta | Discourse |
| Thag. | Theragāthā | Elders' Verses |
| Thīg. | Therīgāthā | Elders' Verses |
| Ud. | Udāna | Verses of Uplift |
| Vbh. | Vibhaṅga | Book of Analysis |
| Vin. | Vinayapiṭaka | Book of the Discipline |
| Vism. | Visuddhimagga | Path of Purification |
| Vv. | Vimānavatthu | Stories of the Mansions |

Milinda's India

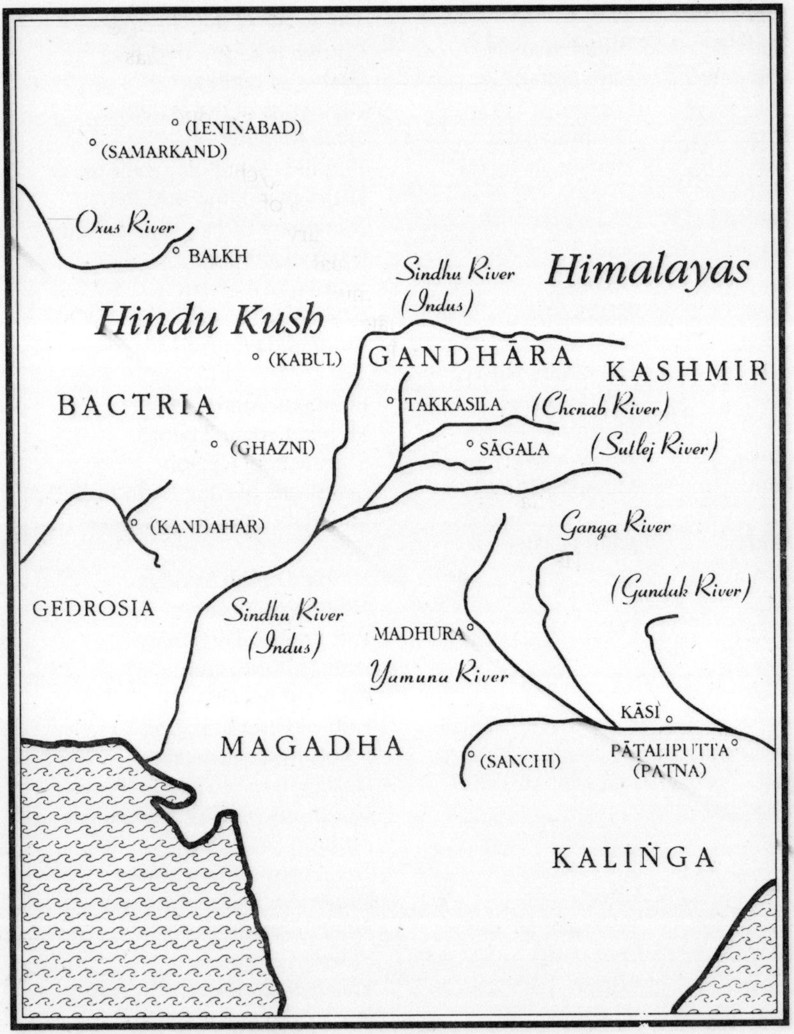

The *Milinda Pañha* is an ancient and much venerated book of the Buddhists, indeed regarded so highly as to be included by the Burmese in the Pali Canon. In the Pali book it says that the conversations between King Milinda and Nāgasena took place five hundred years after the *Parinibbāna* of the Buddha. Mr T.W. Rhys Davids, the most able translator of the Pali texts, regarded the *Milinda Pañha* very highly. He said, "I venture to think that the *'Questions of King Milinda'* is undoubtedly the masterpiece of Indian prose; and indeed the best book of its class, from a literary point of view, that had been produced in any country."[1]

The style of the *Milinda Pañha* is very much like a Platonic dialogue, Nāgasena playing the part of Socrates and winning over King Milinda to the Buddhist view point by his sound reasoning and his fitting similes. The author is not known but it is almost certain that he lived in the far northwest of India or in the Punjab, since he mentions no place in the interior of India south of the Ganges.[1] This is supported by what is definitely known about King Menander, a Bactrian king identified with Milinda.

Much more is known about King Menander. Many of his coins have been found over a wide area of northern India, as far west as Kabul, as far east as Mathura and as far north as Kashmir. The portrait is sometimes of a young man and other times that of a very old man. Plutarch says, "Menander was a king noted for justice who enjoyed such popularity with his subjects that upon his death, which took place in camp, diverse cities contended for the possession of his ashes. The dispute was settled by the representatives of the different cities agreeing to divide the relics, and then erecting separate monuments to his memory".

The recent publication of the Mir Zakah treasure confirms the rule of Menander in Ghazni and adjoining areas of the Kabul valley in the north (there are 521 coins of Menander in that treasure). The discovery of an Attic Tetradrachm of Menander sets speculation at rest; he must

---

[1] T.W. Rhys Davids, QKM introduction.

have ruled over the Kabul region. In the north he occupied Hazara and the Swat valley.[1] So Menander was one of the most important of those Greek kings who continued in Bactria the dominion founded by Alexander the Great. He probably reigned from about 150 to 110 B.C. (thus dating his conversations not much more than 400 years after the *Parinibbāna* of the Buddha). Strabo, draws attention in passing to the remarkable way in which the kingdom of Bactria expanded beyond its original limits, and he mentions incidentally that the kings chiefly responsible were Demetrius and Menander ... But Menander left a far deeper mark on the tradition of India than did Demetrius.[2]

Menander annexed the Indus delta, the peninsula of Surastra (Kathiavar), occupied Mathura on the Jumna, besieged Madyamika (Nagari near Chitor) and Saketam in southern Oudh, and threatened the capital, Pāṭaliputta. But the invasion was repulsed and Menander was forced to return to his own country.[3] Since the Bactrians later became Buddhists there can be little doubt that King Menander is indeed the King Milinda referred to in the book. However, the conversations may be just a literary device the author used to add interest. His primary aim is to clarify Buddhist doctrine and to refute the wrong views promulgated by various opponents of Buddhism.

The introductory story in the *Milinda Pañha* concerning Nāgasena's upbringing is almost identical to the story of the young Moggaliputta Tissa, which is told in the *Mahāvaṃsa,* the Ceylon Chronicles. Moggaliputta Tissa Thera lived about a hundred years before Menander and is mentioned twice in the text [Miln. pp 3,71] so it is probably his story that is the older of the two. However, the *Mahāvaṃsa* was written much later, by Mahānāma at the beginning of the 6th century A.D., so the story could have been borrowed by Mahānāma from the *Milinda Pañha,* which was by then a venerable book edited by Buddhaghosa. (In the *Milinda Ṭika,* a commentary on the *Milinda Pañha,* it is stated that several verses of prologue and epilogue in the *Milinda Pañha* were composed by Buddhaghosa).

---

1 A.K. Narain, *The Indo-Greeks*.

2 Cambridge History of India, Vol. I. p 446.

3 V.A. Smith, The Early History of India.

From the supposed conversation that Milinda has with Pūraṇa Kassapa, Makkhali Gosala and other ascetics[1] it is obvious that this introductory story was fabricated by the author since these ascetics were contemporaries of the Buddha. The story is based on the *Sāmañña Phala Sutta* of the *Dīgha Nikāya*. One point of difference is noteworthy: in the *Sāmañña Phala Sutta,*[2] Prince Ajātasattu goes to see the Buddha but is unable to recognise him; whereas in the introduction to the *Milinda Pañha,* King Milinda says of Nāgasena, "There is no need to point him out to me", thus showing his great superiority to Prince Ajātasattu.

## *The Rise of the Magadha Kingdom*

In the *Mahāparinibbāna Sutta* the Buddha predicted that the city of Pāṭaliputta, which was founded shortly before his death, would become a great city, "Ānanda, among the towns and cities that are centres of congregation and commerce of people of the Aryan race, this new town will become the greatest city called Pāṭaliputta, a place where goods are unpacked, sold and distributed, but it will be in danger from flood, fire and internal dissension".[3] The Magadha Kingdom, of which Pāṭaliputta (modern Patna) was the capital, gradually became the most powerful in all India.

In the mid 4th century B.C. a Sudra named Mahāpadma Nanda usurped the throne of the kingdom of Magadha and became the ruler of a kingdom stretching from the Brahmaputra river in the east to the Beas in the west. But beyond the Beas were several small kingdoms.

During this period, Alexander the Great conquered Persia and crossed the Hindu Kush into Bactria (Northern Afghanistan). It took him two years to subdue these inhospitable regions, but in so doing he founded several cities penetrating as far north as Samarkand and Leninabad (in the USSR). Another city has been identified at Charikar (north of Kabul). Hearing about the river Indus he recrossed the Hindu Kush in 327 B.C. and pushed eastwards to Taxila *(Takkasīla),* but when he reached the Jhelum river he encountered the Paurava rajah who had war elephants. Even the veterans of Macadonia were unable to continue against such opposition so Alexander was forced to retreat

---

1 Though this supposed conversation is found in the original text, it adds nothing of substance to the dialogues, and could not have taken place, so I have left it out.

2 D. i. 50.

3 D. ii. 87, 88.

down the Indus river and thence back through Persia, where he died at Babylon in 323 B.C. Nevertheless, he had left behind him the foundations of the Bactrian kingdom and had surveyed the Jhelum and Indus rivers.

After Alexander's death, Chandragupta, the founder of the Mauryan dynasty, was able to drive away the Greek garrisons from the Indus valley. In 321 B.C. he defeated Nanda and became the ruler of the Magadha kingdom from the capital at Pāṭaliputta. Alexander's successor, Seleukos I Nikator, led an expedition against the Indians in 311 B.C. hoping to regain the Punjab. However, he was up against the might of Chandragupta. So, by 304 B.C., Seleukos was glad to conclude a treaty with him, giving his daughter in marriage and ceding large areas of what is now Baluchistan and Afghanistan in exchange for 500 war elephants. Seleukos sent his ambassador, Magasthenes, to Pāṭaliputta and from what remains of his writings we know something about the size of the army and the strength of the fortifications there. Chandragupta ruled for 24 years and his son Bindusāra, about whom we know very little, ruled for 28 years until his death in 269 B.C.

At the time of Bindusāra's death his eldest son was the viceroy at *Takkasīla* and his younger son, Asoka, was the viceroy at Ujjeni in the south. Asoka fought with his brother for the right to ascend to the throne, and when his brother was killed in battle, Asoka became the ruler of a vast empire from Bengal to Afghanistan. However, he was still not satisfied and it was only in the ninth year of his reign, after the bloody conquest of the Kaliṅga kingdom (Orissa) that he gave up warfare and became a devoted follower of Buddhism. Emperor Asoka sent missions of monks to the border areas of his great empire. Asokan inscriptions have been found in the Kabul valley written in Greek and Aramaic, and elsewhere his inscriptions say that he had made Dhamma conquests in Egypt, Syria, Macedonia, Greece, Cyprus, Bactria, Kashmir, Gandhāra, *etc.* The *Mahāvaṃsa* says that missionaries were sent to Kashmir, Gandhāra, Bactria, the Himalayas, Sindh (Gujarat), and inscriptions on relic caskets found in *stūpas* at Sanchi record the success of those missions to the Himalayas. Unfortunately, the other *stūpa* records have been vandalised, but we can be sure that the missions to Kashmir and Gandhāra were successful since even in the Buddha's time *Takkasīla* was a renowned centre of learning. The

*Mahāvaṃsa* also records that at the consecration of the Great *Stūpa* in 157 B.C. monks came from Alasanda (Charika) in Yona (Bactria).

## *The Rise of the Bactrian Kingdom*

After the death of Asoka in 227 B.C. the Mauryan empire began to disintegrate. The empire founded by Seleukos had already revolted in 250 B.C. under its governor, Diodotus I and it continued to grow under his successors, Diodotus II and Euthydemus. At the beginning of the 2nd century B.C. the Greek rulers of the new kingdom of Bactria crossed the Hindu Kush and began to invade India from the northwest. Of the Greek kings who ruled to the south of the Kush, Apollodotus would seem to be the first. He is twice mentioned in association with Menander. Their rule extended on the south west to Ariana (southern Afghanistan) and in the south to the Indus valley.

As mentioned above, Menander must have ruled over the Kabul and Swat valleys and at some time he annexed the Indus valley too. Sāgala, the city mentioned in the *Milinda Pañha* as the place where the dialogues took place, was the ancient city of the Madras who came to the region in about the 6th century B.C. It is now Sialkot between the Chenab and Ravi rivers, near the border of Kashmir. At Miln. page 83 (see Question 5, Chapter Seven) it is mentioned that Kashmir is 12 *yojanas* (84 miles) distant and that Milinda's birth place on the island of Alasanda is 200 *yojanas* away. There are many cities founded by Alexander during his conquests, several of which might have been the birth place of Menander. The city founded at Charikar has been suggested by A.K. Narain but it is rather less than 200 *yojanas* (1400 miles) at the usual reckoning. Could it perhaps be the Alexandra located at Leninabad or one of the Alexandras further West?

However, from the available evidence we can postulate that Menander was born in Bactria, but brought up in Ariana (the Kabul valley) and in the early years of his rule expanded his father's kingdom to the Indus valley and beyond, perhaps later establishing his capital at Sāgala. Unlike Bactria, which was predominantly influenced by Greek culture, these new areas were already Buddhist. Menander, then, would have been educated in the Greek traditions but would have had direct contact with Buddhism and no doubt often met monks living in his kingdom. Nevertheless, it does seem rather improbable that his knowledge of doctrine would have been sufficient to engage in the dialogues as recorded in the *Milinda Pañha* since Milinda is shown to have a substantial knowledge of the texts. My opinion is that the author had at most a brief acquaintance with Menander, most probably basing his work on an oral tradition of the dialogues and using his own deep knowledge of the texts to extend the dialogues into the longer work that we have now. He might have used the dialogues as a device to add interest to his treatise and to please the Greek king by making him one of the central characters.

This hypothesis gains some support from the existence of Chinese translations that consist of only the first three divisions. They are almost identical with the Pali as to the questions asked but differ in the introductory story, which in neither case looks very authentic.

## *Comparison with the Chinese Text*

As V. Trenchner pointed out when he transliterated the Pali text in the 1860's, we can be sure that the original *Milinda Pañha* was in Sanskrit because it begins with the words *"Taṃ yathā nusuyatā"*(thus has it been handed down) rather than the Pali formula *"Evaṃ me sutaṃ"* (thus have I heard). This is confirmed by the presence of Chinese translations of the text which, although they obviously come from the same root source, show a number of notable differences.[1]

1. The Chinese versions correspond to the first three divisions of the Pali version, suggesting that the other four divisions (Dilemmas, A Question solved by Inference, Ascetic Practices, and the Similes) were later accretions.
2. The Chinese work, the *Nāgasena-bhikshusūtra* takes the name of the monk. The Pali work, the *Milinda Pañha,* the name of the king.
3. The Pali work has twelve extra questions.
4. The stories of the former lives of Nāgasena and Milinda are different.
5. There is no mention of the *Abhidhamma* in the Chinese. It is frequently mentioned in the Pali.

[1] For a detailed and thorough comparison see, *Milinda Pañha* and *Nāgasenabhikshusūtra* (A Comparative Study) Bhikkhu Thich Mihn Chau.

6. On the very well known classification of the *Bodhipakkhiya Dhammas* the Chinese translator goes astray on several terms, indicating that he was not familiar with the Pali texts.
7. The Pali says that animals have reasoning but not wisdom; the Chinese says they have wisdom but their hearts are different.

Although there are many minor differences between the two texts, the close correlation between the similes used to illustrate the terms defined and the order of the questions, leaves us with no doubt that they are both translations of an older work (probably in Sanskrit). However, we should be cautious when drawing conclusions as to which is the more authentic. Bhikkhu Thich Mihn Chau, in his efforts to prove the greater antiquity of the original on which the Chinese translation is based, dates it soon after the demise of the Buddha citing the absence of classification of the texts into *Vinaya, Sutta, Abhidhamma,* and *Nikāyas,* which were only well defined at the Third Council. Yet, Menander was not even born until 100 years after this council. Clearly, the 'original' is not earlier than the 1st century B.C. and the long gap before the translations appeared, in about 400 A.D., was ample time for numerous accretions and amendments, or omissions and lacunas to occur.

For the reasons already stated above and because the conversations in the *Milinda Pañha* were said to have taken place about 500 years after the Buddha's death, whereas Menander lived at least a hundred years earlier than that it seems most likely that the *Milinda Pañha* was composed some time after Menander's death, perhaps being based on an oral tradition of actual conversations that did take place between Menander and a monk or several monks.

Menander's successors, Queen Agathocleia and Strato I Soter, continued to reign for at least 40 years after his death but their lives saw the emergence of a new dynasty in western India, that of the Sakas (Scythians) and Yueh-Chih from central Asia, and the Greek Bactrian era came to an end.

## *The Arrangement of the Pali Book*

The epilogue says that the book is divided into 6 divisions and 22 chapters containing 262 questions, 42 of which have not been handed down making 304 in all, but it is difficult to see how this is reckoned. There are numerous discrepancies between the different texts available, which is to be expected in such an old work. Now only 237 questions remain.

To make cross-reference easier I have followed the same sequence as the Pali text in numbering the questions and chapters, except that I have condensed the last seven chapters into chapter seventeen.

In this edition of the *Milinda Pañha*, although I have followed the arrangement of the Pali text, I have left out large numbers of similes and condensed long, though often very eloquent passages, (without, I hope, spoiling the beauty of the original work) in order to make the book reasonably concise and thus make it more appealing to the busy western reader. It is an abridgement, not a translation, therefore here and there I have combined separate paragraphs into one for the sake of brevity, but I have endeavoured to be faithful to the intention of the original author, which was the clarification of the Buddha's teaching and the elucidation of some common misconceptions that one may fall into.

The references in the footnotes are to page numbers of the **Pali** texts of the Pali Text Society. In the corresponding translations these page numbers are given in square brackets at the top of each left-hand page or; in the case of *Vinaya* and *Jātaka* books, in the body of the text.

To help those who would like to know the Pali word from which its translation derives (which is sometimes different to that used by Rhys Davids or Miss Horner) I have included Pali words in the index alongside the English reference. I have also compiled a list of quotations from the scriptures given by the author of the *Milinda Pañha* and a few other passages found only in *Milinda Pañha*, which might be of interest for further study.

For those unfamiliar with Buddhist terminology I have included a glossary of Pali terms with a brief explanation of their significance.

# THE DEBATE OF KING MILINDA

## Prologue

Milinda was the king in the city of Sāgala. He was learned in the arts and sciences and was of an inquiring disposition. He was skilled in debating and no one could resolve his doubts about religious matters. Though he questioned all the famous teachers none could satisfy him.

Assagutta, one of a large number of *arahants* living in the Himalayas, knew of the king's doubts by means of supernormal power. So he convened an assembly to ask if there was anyone who could answer the king. There was no one, so the whole assembly ascended to the heaven of the thirty-three and requested the god Mahāsena to take birth as a man in order to protect the religion. One of the monks, Rohaṇa, agreed to go to Kajangalā where Mahāsena had been reborn and wait for him to grow up. The boy's father, Brahman Sonuttara, had the boy educated in the three Vedas but the boy, Nāgasena, declared:

> "Empty are these three Vedas and as chaff. There is in them neither reality, worth nor essential truth."

Realising that the boy was ready, Rohaṇa appeared and the parents consented to their son becoming a novice. So, Nāgasena studied the *Abhidhamma*. After gaining perfect knowledge of the seven books of the *Abhidhamma,* Nāgasena was admitted to the Order of monks and Rohaṇa sent him to Vattaniya Hermitage to study with Assagutta. While spending the rainy season there, Nāgasena was asked to preach a sermon to the pious lady who was Assagutta's supporter. As a result of the discourse both the lady and Nāgasena attained the Eye of the Dhamma, the knowledge that whatsoever has a beginning also has the inherent quality of passing away. Assagutta then sent Nāgasena to Dhammarakkhita at the Asoka Park in Pāṭaliputta where, within the space of three months, he mastered the remainder of the *Tipiṭaka*. Dhammarakkhita admonished his pupil not to be content with mere book knowledge and the very same night the diligent pupil Nāgasena gained *arahantship.* He then went to join the other *arahants* who were still staying in the

Himalayas. Having completed his education Nāgasena was ready to meet anyone in debate.

Meanwhile, King Milinda continued his spiritual quest by visiting the *bhikkhu* Āyupāla at the Saṃkheyya Hermitage and asked him why the monks renounced the world. The elder replied, "It is for the sake of being able to live in righteousness and in spiritual calm." Then the king asked, "Is there, venerable sir, any layman who lives so?" The elder admitted that there were many such laymen, and the king retorted:

"Then most venerable Āyupāla, your going forth is of no use. It must be in consequence of sins committed in some former birth that recluses renounce the world and even subject themselves to the added constraints of one or other of the ascetic practices such as wearing only rag-robes, eating only one meal a day, or not lying down to sleep. There is no virtue therein, no meritorious abstinence, no righteousness of life!"

When the king had spoken thus the venerable Āyupāla was silenced and had not a word to say. Then the five hundred Bactrian Greeks who accompanied the king said, "The elder is learned but he is also diffident, so he makes no reply." To this the king replied by exclaiming: "All India is an empty thing, it is like chaff. There is no one who is capable of debating with me and dispelling my doubts!"

However, the Bactrian Greeks were unmoved so the king asked, "Is there then, my good men, any other learned sage who is able to discuss things with me and dispel my doubts?"

Then the minister Devamantiya said, "There is, Great King, an elder named Nāgasena who is learned, of subdued manners yet full of courage; he is capable of discussing with you. He is now staying at this Saṃkheyya Hermitage, you should go and put your questions to him." At the mere mention of the name 'Nāgasena' the king became alarmed and the hairs of his body stood on end. Then the king sent a messenger to say that he was coming. Attended on by the five hundred Bactrian Greeks, the king mounted his royal chariot and went to the place where Nāgasena was staying.

# CHAPTER ONE

## The Soul

King Milinda went up to Nāgasena, exchanged polite and friendly greetings, and took his seat respectfully to one side. Then Milinda began by asking:

1. "How is your reverence known, and what sir, is your name?"

"O king, I am known as Nāgasena but that is only a designation in common use, for no permanent individual can be found."

Then Milinda called upon the Bactrian Greeks and the monks to bear witness: "This Nāgasena says that no permanent individual is implied in his name. Is it possible to approve of that?" Then he turned to Nāgasena and said, "If, most venerable Nāgasena, that is true, who is it who gives you robes, food and shelter? Who lives the righteous life? Or again, who kills living beings, steals, commits adultery, tells lies or takes strong drink? If what you say is true then there is neither merit nor demerit, nor is there any doer of good or evil deeds and no result of *kamma*. If, venerable sir, a man were to kill you there would be no murder, and it follows that there are no masters or teachers in your Order. You say that you are called Nāgasena; now what is that Nāgasena? Is it the hair?"

"I don't say that, great king."

"Is it then the nails, teeth, skin or other parts of the body?"

"Certainly not."

"Or is it the body, or feelings, or perceptions, or formations, or consciousness?[1] Is it all of these combined? Or is it something outside of them that is Nāgasena?"

Still Nāgasena answered: "It is none of these."

"Then, ask as I may, I can discover no Nāgasena. Nāgasena is an empty sound. Who is it we see before us? It is a falsehood that your reverence has spoken."

"You, sir, have been reared in great luxury as becomes your noble birth. How did you come here, by foot or in a chariot?"

---

[1] *See* the glossary.

"In a chariot, venerable sir."

"Then, explain sir, what that is. Is it the axle? Or the wheels, or the chassis, or reins, or yoke that is the chariot? Is it all of these combined, or is it something apart from them?"

"It is none of these things, venerable sir."

"Then, sir, this chariot is an empty sound. You spoke falsely when you said that you came here in a chariot. You are a great king of India. Who are you afraid of that you don't speak the truth?" Then he called upon the Bactrian Greeks and the monks to bear witness: "This King Milinda has said that he came here in a chariot but when asked what it is, he is unable to show it. Is it possible to approve of that?"

Then the five hundred Bactrian Greeks shouted their approval and said to the king, "Get out of that if you can!"

"Venerable sir, I have spoken the truth. It is because it has all these parts that it comes under the term chariot."

"Very good, sir, your majesty has rightly grasped the meaning. Even so it is because of the thirty-two kinds of organic matter[1] in a human body and the five aggregates of being[1] that I come under the term 'Nāgasena'. As it was said by Sister Vajīra in the presence of the Blessed One, 'Just as it is by the existence of the various parts that the word "Chariot" is used, just so is it that when the aggregates of being are there we talk of a being'."[2]

"Most wonderful, Nāgasena, most extraordinary that you have solved this puzzle, difficult though it was. If the Buddha himself were here he would approve of your reply."

2. "How many 'rains'[3] do you have Nāgasena?"

"Seven, your majesty."

"How can you say it is your seven; is it you who are seven or the number that is seven?"

Then Nāgasena said, "Your shadow is now on the ground. Are you the king, or is the shadow the king?"

"I am the king, Nāgasena, but the shadow comes into being because of me."

---

[1] *See* the glossary.

[2] S. i. 135, *see* quotations.

[3] A *bhikkhu's* seniority is reckoned by the number of rainy seasons that have passed since his ordination.

"Just so, O king, the number of the years is seven, I am not seven, but it is because of me that the number seven comes into being and it is mine in the same sense as the shadow is yours."

"Most wonderful, Nāgasena, and extraordinary. Well has this puzzle been solved by you, difficult as it was."

3. Then the king said, "Venerable sir, will you discuss with me again?"

"If your majesty will discuss as a scholar, yes; but if you will discuss as a king, no."

"How is it then that scholars discuss?"

"When scholars discuss there is a summing up and an unravelling; one or other is shown to be in error. He admits his mistake, yet he does not become angry."

"Then how is it that kings discuss?"

"When a king discusses a matter and advances a point of view, if anyone differs from him on that point he is apt to punish him."

"Very well then, it is as a scholar that I will discuss. Let your reverence talk without fear."

"It is well your majesty."

"Nāgasena, I will ask a question", said the king.

"Ask it sir."

"I have asked it, your reverence."

"Then I have answered."

"What have you answered?"

"What have you asked?"

Thinking, "This monk is a great scholar, he is quite able to discuss things with me", the king instructed his minister, Devamantiya, to invite him to the palace with a large company of monks and went away muttering, "Nāgasena, Nāgasena."

4. So, Devamantiya, Anantakāya and Mankura went to Nāgasena's hermitage to accompany the monks to the palace. As they were walking along together Anantakāya said to Nāgasena, "When, your reverence, I say, 'Nāgasena' what is that Nāgasena?"

"What do you think that Nāgasena is?"

"The soul, the inner breath, which comes and goes."

"But if that breath, having gone out, should not return would that man still be alive?"

"Certainly not."

"And when those trumpeters and the like have blown their trumpets does their breath return to them?"

"No venerable sir, it doesn't."

"Then why don't they die?"

"I am not capable of arguing with you sir, pray tell me how it is."

"There is no soul in the breath. These inhalations and exhalations are merely constituent powers of the bodily frame." Then the elder[1] talked to him on the *Abhidhamma* and Anantakāya was satisfied with his explanation.

5. Then, after the monks had arrived at the palace and finished their meal, the king sat down on a low seat and asked, "What shall we discuss?"

"Let our discussion be about the *Dhamma*."

Then the king said, "What is the purpose, your reverence, of your going forth and what is the final goal at which you aim?"

"Our going forth is for the purpose that this suffering may be extinguished and that no further suffering may arise; the complete extinction of grasping without remainder is our final goal."

"Is it, venerable sir, for such noble reasons that everyone joins the Order?"

"No. Some enter to escape the tyranny of kings, some to be safe from robbers, some to escape from debt and some perhaps to gain a livelihood. However, those who enter rightly do so for the complete extinction of grasping."

6. The king said, "Is there anyone who is not reborn after death?"

"Yes there is. The one who has no defilements is not reborn after death; the one who has defilements is reborn."

"Will you be reborn?"

"If I die with attachment in my mind, yes; but if not, no."

7. "Does one who escapes from rebirth do so by the power of reasoning?"

[1] *Thera* (elder) is nowadays normally used only for *bhikkhus* of ten or more years standing but Nāgasena was only seven rains. *See* Question 2 above.

"He escapes both by reasoning and by wisdom, confidence, virtue, mindfulness, energy and concentration."

"Is reasoning the same as wisdom?"

"No. Animals have reasoning but they do not have wisdom."

8. "What, Nāgasena, is the characteristic mark of reasoning; and what the mark of wisdom?"

"Taking hold is the mark of reasoning, cutting off is the mark of wisdom."

"Give me an illustration."

"How do barley reapers reap the barley?"

"They grasp the barley into a bunch with the left hand and, with a sickle in the right hand, they cut the barley."

"Just so, O king, the recluse takes hold of his mind with reasoning and cuts of the defilements with wisdom."

9. "What, Nāgasena, is the characteristic mark of virtue?"

"Supporting, O king, for it is the basis of all good qualities: the five controlling faculties[1] and the five moral powers,[1] the seven factors of enlightenment[2] the eight factors of the noble path,[3] the four foundations of mindfulness[4] the four right efforts,[5] the four bases of success,[6] the four absorptions,[7] the eight freedoms,[8] the four modes of concentration[9] and the eight great attainments.[10] Each of these has virtue as its support and in him who builds on it as the foundation all these good conditions will not decrease."

"Give me an illustration."

---

[1] Confidence, energy, mindfulness, concentration and wisdom.

[2] Mindfulness, investigation, energy, joy, tranquillity, concentration and equanimity.

[3] Right view, ~thought, ~speech, ~action, ~livelihood, ~effort, ~mindfulness, and ~concentration.

[4] Mindfulness of the body, feelings, thoughts, mind-objects.

[5] Effort to prevent and remove unwholesome states and to develop and maintain wholesome states.

[6] Eagerness, energy, tenacity, wisdom.

[7] Four stages of one-pointedness or *jhāna*.

[8] Eight stages of release of the mind by intense concentration.

[9] Meditations on love, compassion, sympathetic joy and equanimity.

[10] Four formless *jhānas* and four form *jhānas*.

"Just, O king, as all forms of animal and plant life flourish with the earth as their support, so does the recluse, with virtue as the support, develop the five controlling faculties and so on.[1] And this was said by the Blessed One:

"When a wise man, established well in virtue,
Develops concentration and understanding,
Then as a *bhikkhu*, ardent and sagacious,
He succeeds in disentangling this tangle."[2]

10. "What is the characteristic mark of confidence?"

"Clarification and inspiration. As confidence springs up in the mind it breaks through the veil of the five hindrances and the mind becomes clear, serene and undisturbed; thus confidence clarifies. Inspiration is the mark when the meditator, perceiving how the minds of others have been set free, aspires to the attainment of what he has not yet reached, to the experience of what he has not yet felt and the realisation of what he has not yet understood. For this was said by the Blessed One:

"By confidence he crosses over the flood,
By vigilance the sea of life,
By steadfastness all grief he stills,
By wisdom he is purified."[3]

11. "What, venerable sir, is the characteristic mark of energy?"

"Reinforcing, O king, so that those good qualities, which it supports, do not fall away."

"Give me an illustration."

"Just as, O king, when his army has been broken up by a larger one the king would call to mind every possible ally to reinforce his army and break up the large army. Thus reinforcing is the mark of energy. For this was said by the Blessed One:

---

[1] *cf.* S. v. 45.

[2] S. i. 13, 165; Vism. (opening verse), *see* quotations.

[3] S. i. 214; Sn. v 184, *see* quotations.

"The energetic noble disciple, O monks,
Puts away unwholesomeness and cultivates good,
Shuns the blameworthy and develops the blameless,
And thus does he keep his mind pure."[1]

12. "What, Nāgasena, is the characteristic mark of mindfulness?"

"Noting and keeping in mind. As mindfulness springs up in the mind of the recluse, he repeatedly notes the wholesome and unwholesome, blameless and blameworthy, insignificant and important, dark and light qualities and those that resemble them thinking, 'These are the four foundations of mindfulness, these the four right efforts, these the four bases of success, these the five controlling faculties, these the five moral powers, these the seven factors of enlightenment, these are the eight factors of the noble path, this is serenity, this insight, this vision and this freedom.' Thus does he cultivate those qualities that are desirable and shun those that should be avoided."

"Give me an illustration."

"It is like a king's treasurer who reminds his master of the size of the army and the amount of wealth in his treasury."

"How is keeping in mind a mark of mindfulness?"

"As mindfulness springs up in the mind, he searches out the categories of good qualities and their opposites thinking, 'Such and such qualities are beneficial and such are harmful'. Thus does he make what is unwholesome in himself disappear and maintain what is good."

"Give me an illustration."

"It is like the Prime Minister of the king who advises him on the right course of action. And this was said by the Blessed One:

"Mindfulness, I declare, O monks,
is helpful everywhere."[2]

13. "What, Nāgasena, is the characteristic mark of concentration?"

"Leading, O king, for all good qualities have concentration as their chief; they incline to it, lead up towards it."

"Give me an illustration."

---

[1] A. iv. 110, *see* quotations.

[2] Untraced, *see* quotations.

"As the rafters of a house incline and lead up to the ridge-pole and the ridge-pole is the highest point of the roof. So too all good qualities incline and lead up to concentration. And this was said by the Blessed One:

> "Monks, develop concentration, a monk who is concentrated sees things as they really are."[1]

14. "What, Nāgasena, is the characteristic mark of wisdom?"

"Illuminating,[2] O king. When wisdom springs up in the mind it dispels the darkness of ignorance, causes the radiance of vision to arise, makes the light of knowledge shine forth and makes the noble truths plain. Thus does the meditator perceive with the clearest wisdom, the impermanence, unsatisfactoriness and soullessness of all formations."

"Give me an illustration."

"It is like a lamp, O king, which in a dark room would illuminate it and make the objects there plainly visible."

15. "These qualities that are so different, Nāgasena, do they bring about one and the same result?"

"They do, the destruction of the defilements of the mind, just as the various parts of an army such as elephants, cavalry, war chariots and archers bring about one result — the conquest of the opposing army."

"Well put Nāgasena, you are clever in reply."

---

[1] S. iii. 13, v. 414; *cf.* Asl.162, *see* quotations.

[2] As well as cutting off already given above.

# CHAPTER TWO

## Rebirth

1. "He who is reborn, Nāgasena, is he the same person or another?"

"Neither the same nor another."

"Give me an illustration."

"In the case of a pot of milk that turns first to curds, then to butter, then to ghee; it would not be right to say that the ghee, butter and curds were the same as the milk but they have come from that so neither would it be right to say that they are something else."

2. "Is the man who will not be reborn aware of the fact?"

"Yes, O king."

"How does he know it?"

"By the cessation of all that is cause or condition of rebirth. As a farmer who does not plough or sow or reap would know that his granary is not getting filled up."

3. "In one, Nāgasena, in whom knowledge *(ñāṇa)* arises does wisdom *(paññā)* also arise?"

"Yes, O king."

"Is knowledge the same as wisdom?"

"Yes, O king."

"Then would he with his knowledge and wisdom be in ignorance about anything?"

"He would still be in ignorance about the things he had not yet learnt but regarding what had been accomplished by wisdom — that is the perception of impermanence, unsatisfactoriness and soullessness — he would not be ignorant."

"Then what would have happened to his delusions on those points?"

"From the moment when knowledge arises, delusion passes away. As when the light comes, darkness disappears."

"But then what has become of his wisdom?"

"When wisdom has accomplished its task then it disappears; but his understanding of impermanence, unsatisfactoriness and soullessness does not disappear."

"Give me an illustration."

"As a man who wants to write a letter at night would have a lamp lit and then write the letter. Then he would put out the lamp, but though the lamp had been put out the letter would remain."

4. "Does he who will not be reborn feel any painful feeling?"

"He may feel physical pain, O king, but not mental pain."

"If he feels painful feelings then why doesn't he just die and attain the extinction of grasping, and put an end to suffering?"

"The *arahant* has no fondness for or aversion to life. He does not shake down the unripe fruit but awaits the time of its maturity. For this was said by Venerable Sāriputta, the Buddha's chief disciple:

"It is not death, nor life I cherish;
As the hireling his wage, so I bide my time.
It is not death nor life I long for,
Mindful and clearly comprehending,
I bide my time."[1]

5. "Is a pleasant feeling wholesome, unwholesome or neutral?"

"It may be any one of the three."

"But surely, venerable sir, if wholesome conditions are not painful and painful ones are not wholesome, then there can be no wholesome condition that is at the same time painful."[2]

"What do you think, O king? If a man were to hold in one hand a hot iron ball and in the other a ball of ice, would they both hurt him?"

"Indeed they would."

"Then your hypothesis must be wrong. If they are not both hot but the heat hurts, and they are not both cold but the cold hurts then the pain does not come from the heat or the cold."

"I am not able to argue with you. Please explain the matter."

---

[1] Thag. 1002, 1003, *see* quotations.

[2] Wholesome deeds are not painful in result but we may find them hard to do because of our attachment and aversion. It is the defilements that cause us to suffer, not the good deeds. Unwholesome deeds are painful in result but we may enjoy doing them due to delusion. When the result comes we have to suffer.

Then the elder taught the king the *Abhidhamma:* "There are six pleasures connected with the world and six of renunciation; six worldly sorrows and six of renunciation; and six neutral feelings in each case, altogether thirty-six. Then there are thirty-six feelings in the past, present and future so altogether there are one hundred and eight feelings."

6. "What is it, Nāgasena, that is reborn?"

"Mind and matter."

"Is it this very mind and matter that is reborn?"

"No, it is not, but by this mind and matter deeds are done and because of those deeds another mind and matter is reborn; but that mind and matter is not thereby released from the results of its previous deeds."

"Give me an illustration."

"It is like a fire that a man might kindle and, having warmed himself, he might leave it burning and go away. Then if that fire were to set light to another man's field and the owner were to seize him and accuse him before the king, and he were to say, 'Your majesty, I did not set this man's field on fire. The fire that I left burning was different to that which burnt his field. I am not guilty'. Would he deserve punishment?"

"Indeed, yes, because whatever he might say the latter fire resulted from the former one."

"Just so, O king, by this mind and matter deeds are done and because of those deeds another mind and matter is reborn; but that mind and matter is not thereby released from the results of its previous deeds."

7. "Will you, Nāgasena, be reborn?"

"What is the use of asking that question again? Have I not already told you that if I die with attachment in my mind I shall be reborn, if not I shall not."

8. "You were explaining just now about mind and matter. Therein what is mind and what is matter?"

"Whatever is gross is materiality, whatever is subtle and mind or mental-states is mentality."

"Why are they not born separately?"

"These conditions are related like the yolk of an egg and its shell, they always arise together and thus they have been related through time immemorial."[1]

9. "Nāgasena, when you say, 'Time immemorial', what does time mean? Is there any such thing?"

"Time means past, present and future. There are some for whom time exists and some for whom it doesn't. Where there are beings who will be reborn, for them time exists; where there are beings who will not be reborn, for them time does not exist."

"Well put Nāgasena, you are clever in reply."

---

[1] Rhys Davids and Miss Horner, using the Sinhalese text, both read this sentence as: *evametaṃ dīghamaddhānaṃ saṃbhāvitaṃ,* which Miss Horner translates, "Thus is produced this long *(saṃsāric)* time". However, the Burmese text has: *sandhāvitaṃ,* and so I have translated accordingly.

# CHAPTER THREE

## The Beginning of Time

1. "What is the root, Nāgasena, of past, present and future time?"

"Ignorance. By ignorance are conditioned formations; by formations, relinking consciousness; by consciousness, mind and matter; by mind and matter, the six sense bases; by the six sense bases, contact; by contact, feeling; by feeling, craving; by craving, attachment; by attachment, becoming; by becoming, birth; by birth are conditioned old age, death, grief, lamentation, pain, sorrow and despair."

2. "You say that the ultimate beginning of things is not apparent. Give me an illustration."

"The Blessed One said, 'By reason of the sense bases and the sense objects there arises contact; by reason of contact, feeling; by reason of feeling, craving; and by reason of craving, action ***(kamma)***. Then, from action, sense bases are once more produced.' Now could there be any end to this series?"

"No."

"Just so, O king, the ultimate beginning of things cannot be comprehended."[1]

3. "Is the ultimate beginning of everything unknown."

"Partly so and partly not."

"Then which so and which not?"

"Whatever condition preceded this birth, that is to us as if it had not been. In reference to that, the ultimate beginning is not known.

---

[1] To search for the origins of life in Super Novae or in DNA is to search in vain for the root cause lies in the mind. The Buddha said:

> "For countless births I wandered in *saṃsāra,* Seeking, but not finding
> the builder of this house. Painful is repeated birth! Housebuilder you
> are seen! You shall build no house again! All your rafters [defilements]
> are broken! Your ridge-pole [ignorance] is shattered!
> My mind has gone to *nibbāna*. Achieved is the end of craving."
>
> Dhp. vv153-4, *see* quotations.

However, that which has not been comes into existence, and as soon as it has arisen it disappears again. With reference to that the ultimate beginning can be known."

4. "Are there any formations that are produced?"

"Certainly, O king. Where there is an eye and also forms there is sight; where there is sight there is contact; where there is contact there is feeling; where there is feeling there is craving; where there is craving there is attachment; where there is attachment there is becoming; where there is becoming there is birth, old age, death, grief, lamentation, pain, sorrow and despair. However, where the eye and forms are not, sight is not; contact is not, feeling is not, craving is not, attachment is not, becoming is not; and where there is no becoming there is no birth, old age, death, grief, pain, sorrow or despair."

5. "Are there any formations that are not produced?"

"There are not, O king, for it is just by a process of becoming that they are produced."

"Give me an illustration."

"Was this house where you are sitting produced by a process of becoming?"

"There is nothing here that was not. This wood was in the forest and this clay was in the ground and it was through the effort of men and women that this house came to exist."

"Just so, O king there are no formations that are not produced."

6. "Is there, Nāgasena, such a thing as 'The one who knows' *(vedagū)?"*[1]

"What is this thing?"

"The living principle within that sees, hears, tastes, smells, feels and discerns things; just as we, sitting here, can look out of any window we wish to."

"If, O king, the living principle within can see, hear, taste, smell and feel things like you say, can it not also see forms through the ear and so on?"

"No, venerable sir."

---

[1] Elsewhere *vedagū* is used as an epithet of the Buddha meaning 'One attained to knowledge'.

"Then, O king, the living principle within cannot make use of whichever sense it pleases as you suggested. It is, O king, by reason of the eye and forms that sight and those other conditions arise, namely; contact, feeling, perception, intention, one-pointedness, vitality and attention. Each arises simultaneously with its cause and herein 'The one who knows' cannot be found."

7. "Does mind-consciousness arise wherever eye-consciousness arises?"

"Yes, O king, where the one is there the other is."

"Which arises first?"

"First eye-consciousness then mind-consciousness."

"Does eye-consciousness issue a command to mind-consciousness or vice versa?"

"No, there is no communication between them."

"Then why is it, Nāgasena, that mind-consciousness arises wherever there is eye-consciousness?"

"Because, O king, there is a tendency, an opening, a habit and an association."

"Give me an illustration."

"If a king's border town had a strong wall and only one gateway and a man wanted to leave the town, which way would he go?"

"Through the gateway."

"And if another man left, which way would he go?"

"Through the same gateway."

"But does the first man issue a command to the second saying, 'Go out the same way as I do', or does the second man tell the first, 'I will go out the same way as you do'?"

"No venerable sir, there is no communication between them."

"In the same way mind-consciousness arises wherever there is eye-consciousness but there is no communication between them."

8. "Where there is mind-consciousness, Nāgasena, is there always contact and feeling?"

"Yes, where there is mind-consciousness there is contact and feeling. And also perception, intention, initial application and sustained application."

"What is the characteristic mark of contact?"

"Touching."

"Give me an illustration."

"As when two rams butt together; the eye is like one ram, visible object is like the other and the butting together of the two is contact."

9. "What is the characteristic mark of feeling?"

"The being experienced, O king, and enjoyed."

"Give me an illustration."

"As a man, who has been of service to a king and has been granted an official post, afterwards enjoys the benefits of being in office."

10. "What is the characteristic mark of perception?"

"Recognising,[1] O king, of blueness, yellowness or redness."

"Give me an illustration."

"It is as the king's treasurer recognises the king's goods on seeing their colour and shape."

11. "What is the characteristic mark of intention?"

"Conceiving, O king, and preparing."

"Give me an illustration."

"As a man having prepared poison and having drunk it would suffer pain, so one having thought out some evil deed and having done it, afterwards has to suffer in hell."

12. "What is the characteristic mark of consciousness?"

"Knowing, O king."

"Give me an illustration."

"As a watchman in the city square would know someone was coming, whichever direction he came from; so, when a man sees an object, hears a sound, smells an odour, tastes a savour, feels a touch or knows an idea; it is by consciousness that he knows it."

13. "What is the characteristic mark of initial application?"

"Fixing, O king."

---

[1] *Saññā, viññāṇa* and *paññā* can be compared respectively to a child, a man and a money-changer who see a gold coin. The child knows it is round and bright but that is all. The man knows that it has a value too. The money-changer knows everything about it. *See* Vism. 437.

"Give me an illustration."

"As a carpenter fixes an accurately cut tenon into a mortice, thus fixing is the characteristic of initial application."

14. "What is the characteristic mark of sustained application?"

"Examining again and again."

"Give me an illustration."

"Like the striking of a gong is initial application; like the reverberation is sustained application."

15. "Is it possible to separate these conditions; saying, 'This is contact, this feeling, this perception, this intention, this consciousness, this initial application, and this sustained application'?"

"No, great king, this cannot be done. If one were to prepare a soup containing curds, salt, ginger, cumin seeds and pepper, one could not take out the flavour of the curds and show it saying, 'This is the flavour of the curds' or take out the flavour of the salt and say, 'This is the flavour of the salt', yet each flavour would be distinctly present by its characteristic sign."

16. Then the elder said, "Is salt, O king, recognisable by the eye?"

"Yes, your reverence, it is."

"Be careful, O king, what you say."

"Then it is recognisable by the tongue."

"Yes, that is right."

"But, Nāgasena, is it only by the tongue that every kind of salt is recognisable?"

"Yes, every kind."

"Then why do bullocks bring whole cartloads of it?"

"It is impossible to bring salt by itself. For example, salt also has mass but it is impossible to weigh salt, one can only weigh the mass."

"You are dexterous, Nāgasena, in argument."

# CHAPTER FOUR

## Sense Bases

1. "Are the five sense bases produced from various *kammas,* or all from one?"

"From various *kammas,* O king."

"Give me an illustration."

"If you were to sow five kinds of seeds in a field the produce would be of five kinds."

2. "Why is it, Nāgasena, that all men are not alike; some are short-lived and some long-lived, some sickly and some healthy, some ugly and some handsome, some powerful and some powerless, some poor and some rich, some low-born and some noble, some foolish and some wise?"

"Why is it that all plants are not alike?"

"Because they come from different seeds."

"Just so, O king, it is because of the variety of *kammas* that beings are not all the same. For this was said by the Blessed One, 'All beings have *kamma* as their own property, are heirs to it, born from it, are relatives of their *kamma* and have *kamma* as their refuge; whatever *kamma* they do divides them into high and low states'."[1]

3. "You said that your going forth was so that this suffering might be extinguished and no further suffering arise. Is it brought about by previous effort, or to be striven after now, in the present?"

"Effort now is concerned with what remains to be done, former effort has accomplished what it had to do."

"Give me an illustration."

"Is it when the enemy is arrayed against you that you set to work to have a moat dug, a rampart raised, a watchtower built, a stronghold constructed and stores collected?"

"Certainly not your reverence."

"Just so, effort now is concerned with what remains to be done, former effort has accomplished what it had to do."

---

[1] M. iii. 203. *cf.* A. v. 87, 288, *see* quotations.

4. "You say that the fire of purgatory would instantly destroy a boulder the size of a house; but you also say that whatever beings are reborn in hell, though they burn for hundreds of thousands of years they are not destroyed. How can I believe this?"

"Although the food, bones and even stones eaten by various female beings are destroyed inside their abdomens yet their embryos are not destroyed. Just so those beings in hell avoid destruction by the influence of their *kamma*."

5. "You say that the world rests on water, the water on air and the air on space. This too I cannot believe."

Then the elder showed the king water in a regulation water-filter supported by atmospheric pressure and the king was convinced.[1]

6. "Is cessation *nibbāna?*"

"Yes, O king. All foolish worldlings take pleasure in the senses and their objects; they find delight in them and cling to them. Hence they are carried down by the flood [of passion] and are not released from birth and suffering. However, the wise disciple of the noble ones does not delight in those things. So craving ceases in him. Thence, attachment ceases, becoming ceases, birth ceases, old age, death, grief, lamentation, pain, sorrow and despair cease to exist. Thus it is that cessation is *nibbāna*."

7. "Does everyone attain *nibbāna?*"

"Not all, O king; but whoever conducts himself rightly, understands what should be understood, perceives what should be perceived, abandons what should be abandoned, develops what should be developed and realises what should be realised;[2] he attains *nibbāna*."

8. "Can one who has not attained *nibbāna* know that it is blissful?"

"Yes indeed, O king. As those who have not had their hands and feet cut off can know how painful a condition it is by the cries of those who have; so can those who have not attained *nibbāna* know it is blissful by hearing the joyful words of those who have attained it."

---

1 *See* note on earthquakes in the glossary.

2 Understands the truth of suffering, perceives impermanence, unsatisfactoriness and not-self, abandons craving, and realises *nibbāna*.

# CHAPTER FIVE

## The Buddha

1. "Have you or your teachers seen the Buddha?"

"No, great king."

"Then, Nāgasena, there is no Buddha!"

"Have you or your father seen the River Ūhā[1] in the Himalayas?"

"No venerable sir."

"Then would it be right to say there is no river Ūhā?"

"You are dexterous, Nāgasena, in reply."

2. "Is the Buddha incomparable?"

"Yes he is."

"But how can you know if you have never seen him?"

"Just as those who have never seen the ocean can know how great it is because the five great rivers flow into it but thereby it does not rise; so do I know that the Buddha is incomparable when I think of those great teachers, whom I have seen, who are only his disciples."

3. "How can others know that the Buddha is incomparable?"

"Long ago there was a master of writing named Tissa Thera.[2] How can people know about him?"

"By his writing."

"Just so, O king, whosoever sees the Dhamma taught by the Blessed One can know that he is incomparable."

4. "Have you, Nāgasena, seen what the truth is?"

"We disciples, O king, have to conduct ourselves according to the rules laid down by the Buddha."[3]

---

[1] The source of the Ganges.

[2] Possibly a reference to Moggalliputta Tissa Thera, the convenor of the Third Council and author of the *Kathāvatthu*, 'Points of Controversy'.

[3] There is a training rule (*Pācittiya* No. 8) preventing monks from disclosing any spiritual attainments.

5. "Can there be any rebirth where there is no transmigration?"

"Yes there can, just as a man can light one oil-lamp from another but nothing moves from one lamp to the other; or as a pupil can learn a verse by heart from a teacher but the verse does not transmigrate from teacher to pupil."

6. Then Milinda asked again, "Is there such a thing as 'The one who knows' *(vedagū)?*"

"Not in the ultimate sense."[1]

7. "Is there any being who transmigrates from this body to another?"

"No there is not."

"If that is so, would there not be an escape from the result of evil deeds?"

"Yes there would be an escape if they were not to be reborn but there would not be if they were to be reborn. This mind and body process commits deeds either pure or impure, and because of that *kamma* another mind and body process is reborn. Therefore this mind and body is not free from its evil deeds."

"Give me an illustration."

"If a thief were to steal another man's mangoes, would he deserve punishment?"

"Indeed he would."

"But the mangoes he stole were not those that the owner had planted; why should he deserve punishment?"

"Because those that he stole resulted from the others."

"Just so, O king, this mind and body process commits deeds either pure or impure, and because of that *kamma* another mind and body process is reborn. Therefore this mind and body is not free from its evil deeds."

8. "When deeds are committed by one mind and body process, where do they remain?"

---

[1] There are two levels of truth; conventional truth and ultimate truth. In the conventional sense it would be wrong to say that a person does not exist; but in the ultimate sense it is right. In reality there is only a continuously changing stream of mind and matter, which we mistake for a person. (Editor's Note).

"The deeds follow them, O king, like a shadow that never leaves. However, one cannot point them out saying, 'Those deeds are here or there', just as the fruits of a tree cannot be pointed out before they are produced."

9. "Would he who is about to be reborn know it?"

"Yes he would, just as a farmer who puts seed into the ground, seeing it rain well, would know that a crop will be produced."[1]

10. "Is there such a person as the Buddha?"

"Yes."

"Can he be pointed out as being here or there?"

"The Blessed One has passed away and nothing remains to form another individual. He cannot be pointed out as being here or there just as the flame of a fire that has gone out cannot be pointed out as being here or there. Yet his historical existence[2] can be known by pointing out the body of the doctrine[3] preached by him."

---

[1] *cf.* Question 2 in Chapter Two.

[2] As well as the existence of more Buddhas in the future.

[3] *Dhammakāya*.

# CHAPTER SIX

## Attachment

1. "Is the body, Nāgasena, dear to you recluses?"
"No great king."
"Then why do you nourish it and lavish attention upon it?"
"We nourish it and care for it as you would care for a wound, not because the wound was dear to you but just so the flesh may grow again. For this was said by the Blessed One:

"This filthy body stinks outright
Like ordure, like a privy's site;
This body men that have insight,
Condemn, is object of a fool's delight.

A tumour where nine holes abide
Wrapped in a coat of clammy hide[1]
And trickling filth on every side,

Polluting the air with stenches far and wide.
If it perchance should come about
That what is inside it came out
Surely a man would need a knout
With which to put the dogs and crows to rout'."[2]

2. "If the Buddha was omniscient why did he lay down the rules for the Order only when the occasion arose?"
"He laid down the rules only when the need arose as a skilled doctor only prescribes medicine when the need arises although he knows all the medicines in advance of a disease arising."

---

[1] Only these latter two lines are in Miln.

[2] Vism. 196. Translation, Bhikkhu Ñāṇamoli.

3. "If the Buddha was endowed with the thirty-two marks of a great man[1] why were his parents not also so endowed?"

"As a lotus that is born in the mud and comes to perfection in the water does not resemble them, so the Buddha was unlike his parents."

4. "Was the Buddha a *Brahmacārin,* a celibate?"

"Yes he was."

"Then he was a follower of Brahmā!"

"Although an elephant's sound is like a heron's he is not a follower of herons. Tell me, great king, is Brahmā one with intelligence *(buddhi)?*"

"Yes."

"Then surely he is a follower of the Buddha!"

5. "Is ordination a good thing?"

"Yes it is."

"But did the Buddha obtain it or not?"

"Great king, when the Buddha attained omniscience at the foot of the Bodhi tree that was for him an ordination; there was no conferring of ordination upon him by others in the way that he has laid down for his disciples."

6. "To whom are tears a cure; to the man who weeps at the death of his mother or to him who weeps due to affection for the truth?"

"The tears of the first, O king, are stained and hot with passion but the tears of the second are stainless and cool. There is a cure in coolness and calm but in heat and passion there can be no cure."

7. "What is the distinction between one who is full of passion and one who is devoid of passion?"

"The one is enslaved, O king, and the other is not enslaved."

"What does that mean?"

"One is in want but the other is not."

"But both of them like good food, neither likes bad food."

"The man who is passionate, O king, eats his food experiencing both the taste and the passion for the taste, but the man without passion experiences only the taste and not the passion arising therefrom."

---

[1] Physical characteristics that are predicted by astrology. See D. ii. 17; M. ii. 136; MilnṬ. 17.

8. "Where does wisdom dwell?"
"Nowhere, O king."
"Then there is no wisdom."
"Where does the wind dwell?"
"Nowhere."
"Then there is no wind!"
"You are dexterous, Nāgasena, in reply."

9. "What is meant by the round of rebirths *(saṃsāra)?*"
"Whoever is born here, dies here and is born elsewhere. Having been born there they die and are born somewhere else."

10. "By what do we remember what was done long ago?"
"By memory *(sati).*"
"Is it not by mind *(citta)* that we recollect?"
"Do you, O king, recollect any business that you have done and then forgotten?"
"Yes."
"Were you then without a mind?"
"No, but my memory failed me."
"Then why do you say that it is by mind that we recollect?"

11. "Does memory always arise subjectively or is it stirred up by suggestion from outside?"
"Both, O king."
"But doesn't that amount to all memory being subjective in origin?"[1]
"If, O king, there were no imparted memory then artisans would have no need of practice or schooling and teachers would be useless, but the contrary is the case."

---

[1] It is not clear to me what is meant here. Perhaps King Milinda is suggesting that since a recollection prompted by another afterwards arises by one's own mental effort it is subjective in origin.

# CHAPTER SEVEN

## MEMORY

1. "In how many ways, Nāgasena, does memory spring up?"

"In seventeen ways,[1] O king. That is to say; by personal experience, as when one like Ānanda can recollect his previous lives (without special development); by outward aid, as when others remind one who is forgetful; by the greatness of some occasion, as when a king remembers his coronation or as one remembers attaining the stage of a stream-winner; by the impression made by benefit, as when one remembers that which gave him pleasure; by the impression made by detriment, as when remembers that which gave him pain; by similarity of appearance, as one remembers one's mother or father or brother or sister on seeing someone like them; by dissimilarity of appearance, as one remembers someone on seeing one unlike them; by the knowledge of speech, as when one is reminded by others; by a sign, as when one recognises a draught bullock by seeing a brand mark; by effort to recollect, as when one is urged again and again; by knowledge of spelling, as one who knows how to write remembers that such a letter follows another; by arithmetic, as when accountants do large sums by their skill with figures; by learning by heart, as reciters of scriptures recollect by their skill in reciting; by meditation, as when a monk recalls his previous lives; by reference to a book, as when kings call to mind a regulation made previously by reference to a book; by a pledge, as when a man recollects by the sight of goods deposited the circumstances under which they were pledged; or by association, as when on seeing or hearing something one remembers other things associated with it."

2. "You say that a man who has lived an evil life for a hundred years can, by thinking of the Buddha at the moment of his death, be reborn among the gods; and that a good man can, by one bad deed, be born in hell. These two things I do not believe."

---

[1] Rhys Davids and I.B. Horner have sixteen here but the Burmese edition of the text has *'sattarasa'* (17) and 17 ways are listed.

"What do you think, O king. Would a tiny stone float on water without a boat?"

"No."

"But even a cartload of stones would float in a boat. So you should think of good deeds as a boat."

3. "Do you monks strive after the removal of past, present and future suffering?"

"No. We strive so that this suffering should cease and no other suffering should arise."

"But is there now, Nāgasena, such a thing as future suffering?"

"No."

"Then you are extremely clever to strive after the removal of it!"

"Have rival kings ever risen up to oppose you, O king?"

"Yes they have."

"Was it only then that you made preparations for battle?"

"Not at all. All that had been done beforehand in order to ward off future danger."

"But is there now, O king, such a thing as future danger?"

"No, venerable sir."

"Then you are extremely clever to strive after the removal of it!"

"Well answered, Nāgasena, you are dexterous in reply."

4. "How far is it to the Brahmā realm?"

"Very far, O king; it would take a rock four months to reach the earth from the Brahmā realm even though it fell 48,000 leagues each day."

"So how can a monk travel there so quickly even by supernormal power?"

"Where were you born, O king?"

"There is an island called Alasanda; I was born there."

"How far is it from here?"

"About two hundred leagues."

"Do you recall any business you did there?"

"Yes I do."

"So quickly you have gone two hundred leagues! Just so, the monk can reach the Brahmā realm at once by supernormal power."

5. The king asked, "If one man were to die and be reborn in the Brahmā realm and at the same moment another man were to die and be reborn in Kashmir which man would arrive first?"

"How far is your home town from here?"

"Two hundred leagues."

"And how far is Kashmir?"

"Twelve leagues."

"Which of them did you recall more quickly?"

"Both the same venerable sir."

"Just so, O king, those men who died at the same moment would be reborn at the same moment."

6. "How many factors of enlightenment are there?"

"Seven, O king."

"By how many factors does one awaken to the truth?"

"By one, investigation of truth, for nothing can be understood without that."

"Then why is it said that there are seven?"

"Could the sword that is in your scabbard cut anything if it was not taken up in the hand?"

"No venerable sir."

"Just so, O king, without the other factors of enlightenment, investigation of truth could not awaken to the truth."

7. "Which is the greater, merit or demerit?"

"Merit, O king. One who does wrong feels remorse and realises his mistake, thereby demerit does not increase. However, one who does merit feels no remorse; and gladness and joy arise, and so rejoicing he will be at ease, being relaxed he will feel contented, being content his mind will be easily concentrated, being concentrated he will see things as they really are. In that way merit increases. So merit is much greater. Demerit is relatively insignificant."

8. "Which is the greater demerit, conscious or unconscious wrong-doing?"

"Unconscious wrong-doing, O king."[1]

---

[1] All wrong-doing is rooted in ignorance, so one who does wrong knowingly will feel remorse and correct himself sooner than one who is deluded (Editor's Note).

"Then we should doubly punish those who do wrong unconsciously."

"What do you think, O king, would a man be more seriously burned if he seized a red-hot iron ball not knowing it was hot than he would be if he knew."

"He would be burned more severely if he didn't know it was hot."

"Just so, O king, it is the same with the man who does wrong unconsciously."

9. "Is there anyone who can physically go to the Brahmā realm or to another continent?"

"Yes, O king, there is. As easily as you can jump a short distance by determining in your mind, 'I will land there', so too one who has developed absorption *(jhāna)* can go to the Brahmā realm."

10. "Are there bones 100 leagues long?"

"Yes there are fish in the ocean 500 leagues long (about 3,500 miles!) who have such bones."[1]

11. "Is it possible to suppress the respiration?"

"Yes it is. As it is possible to stop the snoring of one of undeveloped mind by bending his body, so it is possible for one of well developed mind to suppress the respiration."

12. "Why is the ocean so called?"

"Because it is a uniform mixture of salt and water." *(Sama* = even, *Udda* = water, *Samudda* = ocean).

13. "Why is the ocean all of one taste?"

"Because it has stood for so long."[2]

14. "Is it possible to dissect even the most subtle thing?"

"Yes, O king. Wisdom is able to dissect every subtle thing."

"What is meant by every subtle thing?"

---

[1] The one that got away! *cf.* A. iv. 200.

[2] *cf.* Just as the ocean is of one taste, the taste of salt; so the Dhamma is of one taste, the taste of freedom [from suffering].

"Dhamma[1] is everything subtle. However, not all dhammas are subtle, some are coarse. Subtle and coarse are only concepts. Whatever is divisible can be divided by wisdom. There is nothing else that can dissect wisdom."

15. "These three, Nāgasena, consciousness *(viññāṇa),* wisdom *(paññā)* and the soul *(bhūtasmiṃ jīvo);* are they different in essence or only in name?"

"Knowing, O king, is the mark of consciousness and discrimination[2] is the mark of wisdom. A soul cannot be found."

16. The elder said, "A hard thing has been done by the Blessed One; the distinguishing of all those mental conditions that depend on an organ of sense, showing such and such is contact, such is feeling, such is perception, such is intention and such is the mind *(citta).*"

"Give me an illustration."

"If a man were to take a handful of water from the ocean and tasting it could say, 'This water is from the Ganges, this from the Jumna, this from the Gandak, this from the Sarabhu, and this from the Mahi.' More difficult than this is the distinguishing of those mental states that accompany any one of the senses."

Since it was midnight the king made offerings to Nāgasena and the king said, "Like a lion in a golden cage longs only for freedom, so do I long for the monk's life but I would not live long, so many are my enemies."

Then Nāgasena, having solved the questions put by King Milinda, arose from his seat and returned to the hermitage. Not long after Nāgasena had gone, King Milinda reflected on the questions and answers and concluded, "Everything was rightly asked by me and everything was properly answered by Nāgasena." Back at his hermitage, Nāgasena reflected and concluded in a similar manner.

---

[1] Dhamma here is a technical term meaning phenomenon or state. Elsewhere it also means truth, law, doctrine.

[2] As well as cutting off and illuminating already given above.

# CHAPTER EIGHT

## The Solving of Dilemmas

After pondering the whole night on the discussions he had had with Nāgasena, the king took upon himself eight vows: "For these seven days I will decide no case of law, I will harbour no thought of desire, hatred or delusion. Towards all servants and dependants I shall be humble. I shall watch carefully over every bodily act and my six senses. I shall fill my mind with loving-kindness for all beings."

Then he desired to talk with Nāgasena alone saying, "There are eight places to be avoided by him who wants to discuss deeply: uneven ground where the matter considered becomes scattered, verbose, diffuse and comes to nothing; unsafe places where the mind is disturbed by fear and so does not perceive the meaning clearly; windy places where the voice is indistinct; in secluded places there may be eavesdroppers; in sacred places the subject of discussion may be diverted to the serious surroundings; on a road it may become banal; on a bridge it may become unsteady and wavering; and at a public bathing place it would become a matter of common talk.

"Again there are eight kinds of people, Nāgasena, who are apt to spoil the discussion; the lustful, the angry or deluded man, the proud, the covetous, the sluggard, the man of one idea, and the poor fool — these eight are the spoilers of high argument.

"There are eight causes, Nāgasena, of the development and maturing of intelligence: the advance of years, the growth of reputation, frequent questioning, association with a spiritual guide, one's own reasoning, discussion, association with the virtuous and dwelling in a suitable place. This spot is free from objections to talking matters over and I am a model pupil; I am discreet and my insight is mature.

"These, Nāgasena, are the twenty-five duties of a teacher towards his worthy pupil: he must always protect his pupil, let him know what to cultivate and what to avoid, what he should be earnest about and what neglect. He should instruct him as to sleep, keeping in health, what food to accept or reject, teach him moderation in food, and share with him what he gets in his own almsbowl. He should encourage him when he is discouraged and advise him as to suitable company, villages and monasteries to frequent. He should never indulge in joking or foolish talk with him. Having seen any defect he should be patient with him. He should be diligent, one who fulfils the precepts, worthy of respect and open-hearted. He should regard him as a son, strive to bring him forward, make him strong in knowledge, love him, never desert him in need, never neglect any duty and help him back onto the right path when he stumbles."

"O king, there are these ten qualities of a lay disciple. He should share the joy and sorrow of the Order, take the Dhamma as his guide, delight in giving as far as he is able and should strive to revive the religion if it is in decay. He holds right views and, being one free from the excitement of celebrating festivals,[1] he does not run after another teacher even for the sake of his life. He keeps watch over his thoughts, words and deeds, delights in harmony and is unbiased. As he is no hypocrite he takes refuge in the Buddha, Dhamma and Saṅgha. All of these qualities are present in you hence it is proper and becoming in you that, seeing the decay in the religion of the conqueror, you desire its prosperity. I give you leave to ask me whatever you wish."

## 1. *On Honours Paid to the Buddha*

Then, when leave had been granted, Milinda paid homage and, with his hands joined in reverence, began by asking:

"Venerable Nāgasena, the leaders of other sects say, 'If the Buddha agrees to honour and gifts then he is not entirely free from the world. Therefore any service rendered to him becomes empty and vain.' Tear apart this tangle of wrong-views, solve this dilemma and give insight to the future sons of the Buddha with which to refute their adversaries."

"The Blessed One, O king, is entirely set free and has no attachment to either gifts or honour paid to him."

"Nāgasena, a son may speak in praise of his father, or a father in praise of his son but that is not sufficient grounds to silence the critics."

"Even though the Blessed One has now passed away and cannot be said to accept gifts and honours paid to him yet deeds done in his name are of value and bear great fruit. As a great and mighty wind that

[1] *cf.* A. iii. 206. One of five qualities which lead to one being an outcaste. He is not one who believes in the performance of rituals, or in omens; but he believes in deeds, so he celebrates festivals by observing the eight precepts, listening to the Dhamma and practising meditation.

blew, even so the Blessed One has blown over the world with his love, so soothing, so gentle and so pure. Like men tormented by heat and fever are soothed by a cool wind, so, too, beings tormented by the heat of desire, hatred and delusion are pacified by the sublime teaching of the Blessed One. Although, great king, the Blessed One has entirely passed away, he has left behind his doctrine, his discipline and his precious relics whose value derives from his virtue, concentration, wisdom and freedom. Beings afflicted by the sorrows of becoming can still receive the benefits of these things, as those who have fans can still make a breeze although the wind has subsided.

This was foreseen by the Blessed One when he said, 'It may be Ānanda, that some of you may think, "The word of the master is ended; we have no teacher any more", but you should not regard it so. The Dhamma that has been preached by me and the rules that I have laid down, let them be your teachers when I am gone'.[1]

"Hear another reason, O king. Did you ever hear that the ogre Nandaka, who dared to strike the Elder Sāriputta, was swallowed up by the earth?"

"Yes, venerable sir, that is common knowledge."

"Did Venerable Sāriputta acquiesce in that?"

"Venerable Sāriputta would never agree to any pain being inflicted on a fellow creature for he had rooted out all anger."

"Then, if Sāriputta did not consent to it, why was Nandaka swallowed up by the earth?"

"It was because of the power of his evil deed."

"How many, O king, are those who have been swallowed up by the earth?"

"There are five, venerable sir; Ciñca the Brahmin woman,[2] Suppabuddha the Sākyan[3] Devadatta,[4] Nandaka the ogre,[5] and Nanda the Brahman[6] — these have been swallowed up by the earth."

---

[1] D. ii. 154.

[2] DhA. iii. 178, Commentary on Dhp. v 176. She was persuaded by the Buddha's opponents to accuse him of being her lover.

[3] DhA. iii. 44 f, Commentary on Dhp. v 128. He was the father of Yasodharā and Devadatta and while drunk stood in the road obstructing the Buddha.

[4] DhA. i. 147 f, Commentary on Dhp. v 17. He attempted to kill the Buddha.

[5] Vism. 380. He was the *yakkha* who struck Sāriputta on the head.

[6] DhA. ii. 49, Commentary on Dhp. 69. He was a youth who raped the beautiful nun Upalavaṇṇa, who was an *arahant*.

"And whom, O king, had they wronged?"

"The Blessed One or his disciples."

"Therefore, O king, an act done to the Tathāgata, notwithstanding his having passed away, is nevertheless of value and bears fruit."

"Well has this deep question been explained by you, Nāgasena. You have disclosed that which was hidden, undone the knot, cleared the thicket, refuted the false view and the sectarians have been shrouded in darkness by you, the best of all the leaders of schools."

## 2. *The Omniscience of the Buddha*

"Nāgasena, was the Buddha omniscient?"

"Yes, O king, but the insight of knowledge was not always with him. It depended on reflection."

"Then, Nāgasena, the Buddha could not have been omniscient if his knowledge was reached through reflection."

"I will explain further. There are seven classes of mental ability. Firstly, there are ordinary people[1] *(puthujjana)* who are full of desire, hatred and delusion; untrained in their action, speech and thought; their thinking acts slowly and with difficulty.

"Secondly, there are stream-winners[1] who have attained to right view and rightly grasped the Master's teaching. Their thinking powers are quick and function easily as far as the first three fetters are concerned but beyond that they function slowly and with difficulty.

"Thirdly, there are once-returners[1] in whom desire and hatred are reduced. Their thinking powers work quickly and easily as far as the five lower fetters are concerned but slowly and with difficulty beyond that.

"Fourthly, there are non-returners[1] in whom desire and hatred are eliminated. Their thinking powers work quickly and easily as far as the ten fetters but slowly and with difficulty beyond that.

"Fifthly, there are the *arahants*[1] in whom the floods of sensual desire, desire for rebirth, personality-belief and ignorance have ceased, who have lived the holy life and reached their final goal. Their thinking powers work quickly as far as the range of a disciple is concerned but slowly and with difficulty beyond that.[2]

---

[1] *See* the glossary.

[2] There is no lack in their wisdom, but as regards knowledge of former lives or knowledge of the spiritual faculties of beings there is.

"Sixthly, there are Solitary Buddhas[1] who are dependent on themselves alone, needing no teacher. Their thinking powers work quickly as far as their own range is concerned but as regards that which is exclusively the range of the Perfectly Enlightened Ones their thinking works slowly and with difficulty. Like a man who would readily cross a small river that was on his own property but would hesitate to cross the great ocean.

"Lastly, there are Perfectly Enlightened Buddhas who have all knowledge, are endowed with the ten powers, the four modes of fearlessness, and the eighteen characteristics of a Buddha. Their thinking powers are quickly exercised without sluggishness in any area of knowledge. As a sharp bolt on a powerful crossbow would easily pass through a thin cloth, just so their knowledge is unimpeded and easily outclasses the other six. It is because their minds are so clear and agile that the Buddhas can display the Twin Miracle.[2] From that we may only guess how clear and active their powers are. For all these wonders there is no reason other than reflection that can be asserted."

"Nevertheless, Nāgasena, reflection is carried out for the purpose of seeking out what was not already clear before the reflection began."

"A rich man would not be called poor just because there was no food prepared when a traveller arrived at his house unexpectedly; nor would a tree be called barren when it was fully laden just because no fruit had yet fallen on the ground. So too the Buddha is indeed omniscient although his knowledge is gained through reflection."

## 3. *Devadatta's Ordination*

"If the Buddha was both omniscient and full of compassion why did he admit Devadatta to the Order, since by causing a schism[3] [which only a *bhikkhu* can do] he was thereby consigned to hell for an aeon?[4] If the Buddha did not know what Devadatta would do then he was not omniscient and if he knew then he was not compassionate."

---

1 *See* the glossary.

2 A feat of supernormal power where fountains of fire and water issue simultaneously from each pore of his body.

3 Schism occurs when two groups of four or more monks living within the same boundary recite the *Pātimokkha* separately.

4 *Kappa,* or *Kalpa, see* footnote to Dilemma 10.

"The Blessed One was both omniscient and full of compassion. It was because he foresaw that Devadatta's suffering would become limited that he admitted him to the Order. As a man of influence might have a criminal's sentence mitigated from execution to the cutting off of hands and feet but would not thereby be responsible for the pain and suffering that that man had to undergo, or as a clever physician would make a critical disease lighter by giving a powerful purgative, so did the Buddha reduce the future suffering of Devadatta by admitting him to the Order. After he has suffered for the rest of the aeon in purgatory Devadatta will be released and become a Solitary Buddha by the name of Aṭṭhissara."

"Great is the gift bestowed, Nāgasena, by the Blessed One on Devadatta. The Tathāgata pointed out the road to him when he was lost in the jungle, he gave him a firm foothold when he was falling down a precipice. Yet the reason and meaning for this could only have been pointed out by one as wise as you!"

## 4. *Causes of Earthquakes*

"The Buddha said, Nāgasena, that there are eight causes of a great earthquake.[1] Yet we find that there is a ninth cause also mentioned in the texts. When the Bodhisatta Vessantara fulfilled the perfection of generosity by giving away his wife and children as servants then, too, did the great earth shake. If the former statement of the Buddha is true then the latter is false."

"Both statements, O king, are correct. The gift of Vessantara was not mentioned as a ninth cause of a great earthquake because it is an extremely rare occurrence. Just as the dried up creek that does not usually hold water is not called a river, but in times of exceptional rainfall it becomes a river, so too the largesse of Vessantara was an isolated and extraordinary occurrence, and for that reason one distinct from the eight usual causes of a great earthquake.

"Have you ever heard, O king, in the history of our religion of any act of devotion that gave its result in this very life?"

"Yes, venerable Nāgasena, there are seven such cases: Sumana the garland maker,[2] Ekasāṭaka the brahman,[3] Puṇṇa the farm worker,[4]

---

[1] D. ii. 107; A iv. 312, *see* glossary and quotations.

[2] DhA. ii. 40f, Dhp. v 68.

[3] DhA. iii. 1, Dhp. v 116.

[4] DhA. iii. 302f, Dhp. v 223.

Mallikā the queen,[1] the queen known as the mother of Gopāla,[2] Suppiyā the devoted woman[3] and Puṇṇā the slave-girl."[4]

"But have you ever heard, O king, of the earth shaking even once or twice when a gift had been given?"

"No, venerable sir, I have never heard of that."

"I too, O king, have never heard of such a thing, though I have been devoted to study and ready to learn, except for this case of the splendid gift of Vessantara. It is by no common effort, O king, that the great earth is moved. It is when overburdened by the weight of righteousness, overpowered by the burden of the goodness of acts that testify to absolute purity; that, unable to support it, the broad earth quakes and trembles. When Vessantara gave his gift, O king, he was giving things away not for the sake of a glorious rebirth, nor for future wealth, nor to receive gifts in return, nor for flattery, nor for any other personal gain, but only for the sake of supreme wisdom."

## 5. *Asseveration of Truth*

"King Sīvi gave his eyes to someone who begged for them and new eyes arose in their place.[5] How is this possible?"

"It was by the power of the truth that it happened. As when mystics recite the truth they can make the rain fall, drive back fire or neutralize poison.

"When Asoka the righteous ruler stood one day among the townsfolk of Pāṭaliputta he said to his ministers; 'Is there anyone who could make this great Ganges flow backwards and upstream?' Then a certain courtesan, named Bindumatī, was in the crowd and she performed an act of truth. At that very moment the mighty Ganges, roaring and raging, rolled back upstream in sight of everyone. The king, awestruck, sought out the woman who was the cause of this and asked her, 'What is the act of truth by which you did this?' She replied, 'Whoever pays me, whether he is a brahman, a noble, a tradesman or

---

[1] Jā. iii. 405, Dhp. v 177.

[2] AA. i. 207f.

[3] Vin. i. 217-8. Having promised meat broth to a monk she was unable to buy any meat so she cut a piece from her own thigh prepared broth and offered it to the monk. When the Buddha met her the wound healed miraculously. *See also* Dilemma 73.

[4] DhA. iii. 321, Dhp. v 226.

[5] Jā. No. 499.

a servant, I regard them all alike. Free from bias I do service to him who has paid me. This is the basis of the act of truth[1] by which I turned the Ganges back.'

"There is no ordinary cause for those things to happen but the power of truth is itself the cause. And there is no reason for the realisation of the Four Noble Truths other than the power of truth."

## 6. *The Dilemma Regarding Conception*

"The Blessed One said, Nāgasena, that there is conception in a womb with the coincidence of three causes; coitus of the parents,[2] the mother's season and a being to be born.[3] However, he also said that when the ascetic Dukāla touched the navel of the ascetic woman Pārikā with his thumb the boy Sāma was conceived.[4] If the first statement is true then the latter must be false."

"Both statements are true, O king, but you should not think that there was any transgression in the latter case. Sakka, the king of the gods, having seen that those virtuous ascetics would become blind, entreated them to have a son. However, they would not consent to intercourse even to save their lives, so Sakka intervened by instructing Dukāla and thus Sāma was conceived."

## 7. *The Duration of the Religion*

"After the ordination of women, the Blessed One said that the pure doctrine would only last for five hundred years.[5] However, to Subaddha he said, 'So long as the brethren live the perfect holy life then this world will not be bereft of *arahants*.[6] These statements are contradictory."

"O king, the Blessed One did make both statements, but they are different in the spirit and in the letter. One deals with the duration of the pure doctrine whereas the other deals with the practice of the religious life, two things widely distinct. In saying five hundred years

---

[1] There are many examples in the *Jātaka, e.g.* Jā. i. 214, 215. It is not necessary for the truth averred to be commendable. *cf.* Jā. iv. 31-33.

[2] *See* Jā. Nos. 497, 523, 526; and Vin. iii. 205f for examples of conception without sexual intercourse.

[3] M. i. 265, M. ii. 157.

[4] Jā. No. 540.

[5] The Sri Lankan text gives an alternative reading of 5,000 years, *see* quotations.

[6] *See* quotations.

he was fixing a limit to religion but in speaking to Subaddha he was declaring in what religion consisted. If the sons of the Buddha continue to exert themselves in the five factors of striving,[1] have a sincere desire for the three trainings,[2] perfecting themselves in conduct and virtue; then the glorious teaching of the Conqueror will long endure and stand more and more steadfast as the years roll on. The teaching of the Master, O king, has its root in practice, practice is its essence, and it stands as long as practice does not decline.

There are three modes of disappearance of a teaching. The decline of the attainment to a clear insight into it, of practice in accordance with it, and decline in the outward form of it. When the intellectual grasp ceases then even the man who conducts himself rightly has no clear understanding of it. By the decline of practice, promulgation of the *Vinaya* rules ceases and only the outward form of the religion remains. When the outward form ceases then the succession of the tradition is cut off."

## 8. *Purity of the Buddha*

"If the Tathāgata destroyed all unwholesomeness in himself when he gained omniscience why did he get hurt by a splinter of rock that was thrown by Devadatta? If he did get hurt then he cannot have been free from all evil, for there is no feeling without *kamma*. All feeling has its root in *kamma* and it is only on account of *kamma* that feeling arises."

"No, great king, not all feeling has its root in *kamma*. There are eight causes of the arising of feelings. Excess of wind, of bile and of phlegm, the mixture of the three bodily fluids, variations in temperature, stress of circumstances, external agency and *kamma*. Whoever says, 'It is only *kamma* that oppresses beings', thereby excludes the other seven reasons and that statement of theirs is wrong.

"When one's wind is disturbed it happens in one of ten ways; by cold, by heat, by hunger, by thirst, by over-eating, by standing too long, by over exertion, by running, by medical treatment, or as a result of *kamma*. When the bile is disturbed it is in one of three ways; by cold, by heat or by unsuitable food. When the phlegm is disturbed it is in one of three ways; by cold, by heat or by eating and drinking. When these three disturbed fluids are mixed it brings about its own distinctive pain. Then there are

---

[1] *Padhāna* — Confidence, good health, honesty, energy and wisdom.

[2] *Sīla, samādhi, paññā* (Virtue, concentration and wisdom).

pains arising from variations in temperature, stress of circumstances and by external agencies. There is also that pain which has *kamma* as its cause. So the pain that is due to *kamma* is much less than that due to other causes. The ignorant go too far when they say that everything that is experienced is produced as the fruit of *kamma*. Without a Buddha's insight no one can ascertain the extent of the action of *kamma*.

When the Blessed One's foot was grazed by the splinter of rock the pain was produced only by external agency. Although the Blessed One never suffered pain that was the result of his own *kamma*, or brought about by the stress of circumstances, he suffered pain from each of the other six causes.[1]

It was said, O king, by the Blessed One, 'There are certain pains, Sīvaka, which arise from bilious humours and you ought to know what they are for it is a matter of common knowledge. Those ascetics and Brahmans who are of the opinion and proclaim the view that all feelings that men experience are due to a previous act, go beyond certainty and knowledge and therein I say that they are wrong'."[2]

## 9. *Perfection of the Buddha*

"If the Tathāgata had accomplished everything under the bodhi tree why did he spend a further three months in solitude?[3] If a man has eaten and is satisfied, what is the use of further food; if a man is healthy, what is the use of him taking medicine?"

"O king, solitary meditation has many benefits. All the Tathāgatas attained to Buddhahood thereby and practised it in appreciation of its benefits to mankind. There are twenty-eight benefits of solitude:[4] it guards him, increases his life expectancy, gives him vigour, conceals his failings, removes any bad reputation and brings fame, destroys discontent and brings satisfaction, banishes fear and endows him with confidence, removes sloth and fills him with zeal, takes away desire, hatred and delusion, subdues pride, disrupts discursive thought and makes the mind

---

[1] This is a controversial point. There are several references to the Buddha experiencing the result of previous *kamma* collected at Ap. i. 299ff (Editor's Note).

[2] S. iv. 230f, *Moliya Sīvaka Sutta*.

[3] Between the enlightenment *(Vesākha)* and the first sermon *(Asāḷha)* there are only two months but there was an occasion when the Buddha spent three months in solitude. *cf.* Commentary to Dhp. v 6.

[4] *See* quotations.

one-pointed, softens his mind and makes him light-hearted, makes him serious, brings him material gain, makes him worthy of reverence, brings him joy, fills him with delight, shows him the true nature of all formations, puts an end to rebirth, and gains for him all the fruits of a life of renunciation. It is because the Tathāgata has in mind these manifold benefits that he follows the practice of seclusion.

"There are altogether four reasons why the Tathāgatas devote themselves to solitude. For the sake of dwelling at ease, because of its blameless qualities, because it is the way to all noble things without exception, and because it has been praised and exalted by all the Buddhas. It is not because they have anything left to achieve or anything to add to what they have already accomplished but only because of these excellent advantages that they practice seclusion."

## *10. Equanimity of the Buddha*

"The Buddha said that, if he wished, he could live for the remainder of the aeon[1] but he also said that he would die at the end of three months.[2] How can both of these statements be true?"

"Aeon, O king, in that connection means a man's life-span and what the Buddha said was in order to exalt the bases of success *(iddhipāda)*. The Blessed One was entirely free from desire for any kind of future life and condemned them all for he said, 'I find no beauty in the smallest part of future life, just as even a small quantity of excrement is of bad smell'."[3]

---

[1] D. ii. 103. — An aeon or *Kalpa* usually refers to a period of evolution and dissolution of the world but here it means a man's average life-span; about 100 years at the time of the Buddha, now only 75 years. It is said to be reducing by one year every century, *see* quotations.

[2] D. ii. 119, *see* quotations.

[3] A. i. 34, *see* quotations.

## CHAPTER NINE

### THE SOLVING OF DILEMMAS (Contd.)

### 11. *The Minor and Lesser Precepts*

"It has been said by the Blessed One, 'It is from higher knowledge, O monks, that I teach Dhamma.'[1] Yet he also said, 'When I am gone, Ānanda, let the Order if it should so wish, abolish the minor and lesser precepts.'[2] Were then those precepts laid down in error and without due cause?"

"When the Blessed One, O king, said, 'Let the Order abolish the lesser and minor precepts', it was said in order to test the monks. As a king on his death bed would test his sons saying, 'The outer regions of my kingdom will be in danger of falling after my death.' Then would his sons on the death of their father give up those outlying districts?"

"No indeed, venerable sir. Kings are grasping. The princes might, in their lust for power, subjugate an area twice what they already had but they would never willingly give up what they possessed."

"Just so, O king, the sons of the Buddha, in their enthusiasm for the Dhamma might keep even more than one hundred and fifty[3] regulations but they would never give up any that had been laid down."

"Venerable Nāgasena, when the Blessed One referred to the 'Minor and Lesser Precepts' people might be in doubt as to which these were."

"Those acts of wrong-doing[4] are the lesser precepts, and wrong speech[5] refers to the minor precepts. The elders who convened the First Buddhist Council were also not unanimous about this matter."

### 12. *The Esoteric Teaching*

"The Blessed One said to Ānanda, 'In respect of the Dhamma the Tathāgata does not have the closed fist of a teacher who holds something back.'[6] Yet when he was questioned by Māluṅkyāputta he

---

[1] A. i. 276 *cf.* M. ii. 9, *see* quotations.

[2] D. ii. 154; Vin. ii. 287, *see* quotations.

[3] Excluding the 75 minor training rules there are 152 precepts.

[4] *Dukkaṭa*: Transgressions against the 75 training rules and other minor regulations.

[5] *Dubbhāsita*: Frivolous or sarcastic speech that does not amount to lying or abuse of a monk.

[6] D. ii. 100; S. v. 153, *see* quotations.

made no answer.[1] Was it because of ignorance that he did not reply or did he wish to conceal something?"

"O king, it was not because of ignorance, nor for the sake of concealing anything that he did not answer. A question may be answered in one of four ways: directly, with an analysis, with a counter-question or by setting it aside.

"And what sort of question should be answered directly?

'Is matter impermanent? Is feeling impermanent? Is perception impermanent?' These should be answered directly.

"And what should be answered with an analysis?

'Is what is impermanent, matter?'

"And what should be answered with a counter-question?

'Can the eye perceive all things?'

"And which should be set aside?

'Is the world eternal? Is the world not eternal? Does the Tathāgata exist after death? Does he not exist after death? Is the soul the same as the body? Is the body one thing and the soul another?' It was to this sort of question that the Blessed One gave no reply to Māluṅkyāputta. There was no reason to answer it. The Buddhas do not speak without reason."

## 13. *The Fear of Death*

"The Blessed One said, 'All tremble at punishment, all are afraid of death.'[2] Yet he also said, 'The *arahant* has passed beyond all fear.'[3] How is it then? Do the *arahants* tremble at the fear of death? Or are the beings in hell afraid of death by which they may gain release from torment?"

"O king, it was not with regard to *arahants* that the Blessed One said, 'All tremble at punishment, all are afraid of death.' An *arahant* is an exception to that statement for all cause of fear has been removed by him. Suppose, O king, a king had four chief ministers who were faithful and trustworthy; would they be afraid if the king were to issue an order saying, 'All the people in my realm must pay a tax'?"

"No, Nāgasena, they would not be afraid because the tax does not apply to them, they are beyond taxation."

---

[1] M. ii. Sta. 63.

[2] Dhp. v 129, *see* quotations.

[3] *cf.* A. ii. 172, *see* quotations.

"Just so, O king, the statement, 'All tremble at punishment, all fear death', does not apply to *arahants* because they are beyond the fear of death. There are these five ways, O king, in which the meaning of a statement should be established: by comparison with the text quoted; by 'taste' *i.e.* is it in accordance with other texts?; is it in accordance with the word of the teachers?; having considered his own opinion, *i.e.* is it in accordance with my own experience?; and, fifthly, by a combination of all these methods."

"Very well, Nāgasena, I accept that *arahants* are an exception to that statement, but surely those beings in hell cannot be afraid of the death by means of which they will gain release from that torment?"

"Those in hell are afraid of death, O king, for death is a condition that all those who have not seen the Dhamma are afraid of. Suppose, O king, a man kept prisoner in a dungeon were to be sent for by the king who wished to set him free. Wouldn't that prisoner be afraid of meeting the king?"

"Yes he would."

"Just so, O king, those beings in hell are afraid of death even though they will attain release from their torment."

## *14. Protection from Death*

"It was said by the Blessed One, 'Not in the sky, not in the ocean's midst, not in the most secluded mountain cleft, not in the whole wide world is found the spot where remaining one could escape the snare of death.'[1] Yet, on the other hand, the protection verses *(paritta)* were prescribed by the Buddha for the protection of those in danger. If there is no escape from death then the *Paritta* ceremony is useless."

"*Paritta* verses, O king, are meant for those who have some portion of their life remaining. There is no ceremony or artificial means for prolonging the life of one whose life-span has come to an end."

"But, Nāgasena, if he who has a term of life yet to run will live, and he who has none will die, then medicine and *Paritta* are alike useless."

"Have you ever seen or heard of a case of a disease being cured by medicine?"

"Yes, hundreds of times."

---

[1] Dhp. v 128, *see* quotations.

"Then your statement as to the ineffectiveness of *Paritta* and medicine must be wrong."

"Venerable Nāgasena, is *Paritta* a protection to everybody?"

"Only to some, not to all. There are three reasons for the failure of *Paritta:* the obstruction due to past *kamma,* that caused by present defilements, and the obstruction caused by lack of confidence. That which is a protection to beings loses its power through their own blemishes."

## 15. *The Power of Māra*

"Although you say that the Tathāgata was in constant receipt of alms[1] yet when he entered the Pañcasāla village he received nothing due to the intervention of Māra.[2] Is the power of Māra greater than the power of the Buddha or the power of demerit greater than the power of merit?"

"Great king, although what you said is true it is not enough reason to prove your assertion. Consider a gatekeeper at a royal palace. He might prevent someone from bringing a present for the king out of jealousy yet the king would not thereby be less powerful than the gatekeeper. There are four modes of obstructing a gift: to a gift not intended for any particular person, to one set aside for someone, to one being prepared for someone and to the enjoyment of a gift given to someone. In the case you mentioned the gift was not intended specifically for the Blessed One: if it had been no one could have obstructed it.

"There are four things, O king, connected with the Tathāgatas, to which no one can do any harm: the alms intended for him, the halo that surrounds him for one fathom, his omniscience and his life. These things are free from defect and unassailable by other beings and cannot be harmed. When Māra possessed the householders of Pañcasāla village it was as when robbers, by hiding in inaccessible places, beset the highways. However, if the king caught sight of them do you think they would be safe?"

"No, sir, he might have them cut to pieces."

"Just so, O king, if Māra had raised any obstruction to alms intended for the Blessed One his head would have split into a thousand pieces."

---

1 *cf.* A. ii. 87. "I, monks, enjoy a plentiful supply of alms when invited." *See* quotations.

2 S. i. 113 f; DhA. iii. 257, *see* quotations. Māra, as well as being the personification of evil, is a being who was an antagonist of the Buddha and appeared several times during his life to taunt him.

## 16. *Knowledge of Wrong Doing*

"This was said by the Blessed One, 'Whoever ignorantly deprives a living being of life accumulates great demerit.'[1] Yet in the training rule for monks concerning killing living beings he says, 'There is no offence if he does not know.'[2] How can both of these statements be true?"

"There are offences where there is no escape for one who does not know and there are offences where there is an escape.[3] It was in regard to this second kind of offence that the Blessed One said there is no offence if he does not know."

## 17. *The Buddha Is Not Possessive*

"The Blessed One said, 'The Tathāgata does not think that he should lead the Order or that it is dependent upon him.'[4] Yet regarding Metteyya Buddha he said, 'He will be the leader of an Order of several thousands as I am now the leader of an Order of several hundreds'."[5]

"O king, the sense in one passage is inclusive, in the other it is not. It is not the Tathāgata who seeks after a following but the followers who seek after him. It is merely a common opinion that 'This is mine', it is not an ultimate truth. Affection is a frame of mind put away by the Tathāgata; he has put away possessiveness, he is free from the delusion 'This is mine', he lives only to help others. Just as a mighty rain cloud, O king, pours out its rain, and gives sustenance to grass and trees, to cattle and to men, and all living things depend on it but the cloud has no feelings of longing with the idea that 'These are mine' — so too, the Tathāgata instructs all beings in good qualities and maintains them in goodness, and all beings depend on him but he has no concept of possession because he has abandoned all wrong views of self."

---

[1] The quotation given is taken out of context. There is no demerit at all in killing living beings unknowingly (as a blind man walking on ants). Hence I have said 'ignorantly' meaning he kills not knowing it is an unwholesome act which has evil results. *See* Question 8, Chapter Seven. *See also* quotations.

[2] Vin. iii. 78; iv. 49, *etc. See* quotations.

[3] Compare, for example, *Pācittiya* 51; in which taking intoxicants is an offence even if one does not know; to *Pācittiya* 62 where using water with living organisms in it is an offence only if he knows.

[4] D. ii. 100; *cf.* M. i. 459 (MLS. ii. 132), *see* quotations.

[5] D. iii. 76, *see* quotations.

## 18. *The Unity of the Order*

"You say that the Order of the Tathāgata could never be broken up.[1] Yet Devadatta was able to lead away five hundred monks from the Blessed One".[2]

"It was due to the power of the schismatic that the schism occurred for even a mother can be disunited from her son where there is one to make a rift. However, it was said in a special sense that the Order of the Tathāgata could not be broken up. It is an unheard of thing that his following could be disunited by anything done or any unkind word, wrong action or injustice whatsoever of the Tathāgata himself. In that sense his following is invulnerable."

---

[1] D. iii. 172, *see* quotations.

[2] Vin. ii. 198, *see* quotations.

## CHAPTER TEN

### THE SOLVING OF DILEMMAS (Contd.)

### *19. Dhamma is Best*

"It was said by the Blessed One, 'For it is the Dhamma, O Vāseṭṭha, which is the best in the world.'[1] Yet you say that the devout layman who has gained stream-entry ought to pay respect to a novice even though he has no such spiritual attainment. If the Dhamma is indeed best then that custom is inappropriate."

"O king, there is a reason for that custom. There are twenty personal qualities[2] and two outward signs that entitle a recluse to respect. He rejoices in the excellent Dhamma, he has the highest kind of self-control, he has good conduct, because of his mode of living [on alms], he is abstemious, he restrains his senses, he is patient, he is gentle, he lives alone, he delights in solitude, he delights in meditation, he is endowed with shame and fear of wrong-doing, he is energetic, he is earnest, he undertakes the precepts, he recites the scriptures, he questions the learned about the meaning, he delights in virtue, being homeless he is free from worldly attachments, he fulfils the precepts, and he has the two outward signs — a shaven head and the yellow robe. In the practice and development of all these things a recluse lives. By undertaking this training and developing the virtues of a recluse he is progressing towards *arahantship*. Thus, because he sees him as in the company of the most worthy ones, the devout layman thinks it right and proper to revere the recluse though he may be just an ordinary person. Moreover, O king, because he sees him as one who is maintaining the monastic traditions, so too does the devout layman pay respect to the recluse. If a layman attains *arahantship*, only two destinations await him; either he must enter the Order that very day or else he must attain *parinibbāna*.[3] Immovable, O king, is the state of renunciation, glorious and most exalted the condition of being a member of the Order of the Blessed One."

---

[1] D. iii. 93, *see* quotations.

[2] *See* quotations.

[3] Untraced, *see also* Dilemma 62.

## *20. The Compassion of the Buddha*

"You say that the Tathāgata protects beings from harm and blesses them with goodness,[1] yet when the Blessed One was preaching the discourse on the simile of the great mass of fire[2] to the monks, hot blood was ejected from the mouths of sixty monks. By his delivery of that discourse they came to harm and not good so that statement of yours is wrong."

"What happened to them was of their own doing."

"But, Nāgasena, if the Tathāgata had not delivered that discourse would they have vomited hot blood?"

"No. When they took wrongly what was said the burning was kindled within them."

"Then it must have been that the Tathāgata was the chief cause to destroy them. If a snake were to crawl into an anthill, and a man in want of earth were to break into it and take the earth away, and so the snake was to die for want of air, would not the snake have been killed by that man's action?"

"Yes, O king. Nevertheless, when the Tathāgata delivered a discourse he never did so with malice but preached totally free from malice. Those who were practising rightly were enlightened, but those were practising wrongly, fell. Just, O king, as when a man shakes a mango tree, those fruits that are strongly fastened to it remain undisturbed but those that have rotten stalks fall to the ground."

"Then did not those monks fall because of the discourse?"

"Could a carpenter by doing nothing to a piece of timber and simply laying it aside, make it straight and fit for use?"

"No venerable sir."

"Just so, O king, the Tathāgata could not, by merely watching over his disciples, have opened the eyes of those who were ready to see. However, by getting rid of those who took his words wrongly he saved those who were prepared to be saved, and it was because of their own defects that the evil-minded fell."

## *21. The Modesty of the Buddha*

"This too was said by the Blessed One:

---

[1] Untraced but *cf.* A. i. 20, *see* quotations.

[2] A. iv. 128-135, *see* quotations.

"Control of the body is good,
Good is control of speech,
Control of the mind is good,
Good is control in everything."[1]

"Yet when the Tathāgata was seated in the midst of the four congregations [monks, nuns, laymen and laywomen] he showed to Brahman Sela what should not be shown in public — the male organ concealed in a sheath.[2] If he did so then the first statement is false."

"The Blessed One did show to Sela the Brahman what should not be shown in public but it was by means of supernormal power that he created an image of it and only Sela saw that image. To him, in whom doubts had arisen about the Tathāgata, the Master showed the male organ concealed in a sheath by means of supernormal power for the sake of awakening him to the truth. Skilled in means, O king, was the Tathāgata. For the sake of scorning physical beauty the Master took Venerable Nanda to the celestial realm to see the lovely maidens there[3] and by means of a piece of clean white cloth did he awaken Venerable Cūḷapanthaka to the impurity of the body."[4]

## 22. *The Perfect Speech of the Buddha*

"Sāriputta the chief disciple said, 'The Tathāgata is perfect in speech, there is no fault of speech in the Tathāgata concerning which he should have to take care that no one else should know it.'[5] So why did the Buddha use harsh and abusive words to Sudinna the Kalanda and call him a stupid fellow?"[6]

"That was not out of rudeness, O king, but merely to show him the foolish and contemptible nature of his conduct in a way that would do him no harm. If any man in this birth does not attain to perception of the Four Noble Truths, his life has been in vain. The Blessed One used words of

---

[1] S. i. 73; Dhp. v 361, *see* quotations.

[2] M. ii. Sta. 92; Sn. 103. This refers to one of the marks of the Buddha predicted by astrology. Not being able to see this, Sela was still in doubt. *See* quotations.

[3] Jā. ii. 92-94.

[4] Jā. i. 116ff.

[5] D. iii. 217, *see* quotations.

[6] Vin. iii. 20, *see* quotations. The rule forbidding sexual intercourse was laid down because Sudinna was persuaded by his former wife to preserve the family line. Notably, because he was the first offender, he was allowed to remain a monk after his offence.

truth, they were no exaggeration. He admonished others only to destroy the disease of unwholesomeness. His words, even when stern, softened men's pride and made them humble. They were full of compassion and aimed at benefit as the words of a father to his children."

## 23. The Talking Tree

"The Tathāgata said:

> "Brahman! Why do you ask an unconscious thing,
> which cannot hear you, how it is today?
> Active, intelligent and full of life, how can you speak to
> this so senseless thing, this wild Palāsa tree?"[1]

"Yet, on the other hand, the Tathāgata said:

> "And thus the aspen tree made reply,
> 'I, Bhāradvāja, can speak too. Listen to me.'[2]

"If, Nāgasena, a tree is an unconscious thing then this latter statement must be false."

"When the Blessed One said, 'aspen tree' it was just a conventional way of speaking, for though a tree being unconscious cannot speak, the word 'tree' was used as a designation for the deity who dwelt in it and this is a well known convention. Just, O king as a wagon laden with corn is called a 'corn-wagon' though it is not made of corn, it is made of wood. The Tathāgata, when expounding the Dhamma, did so by means of the common mode of speech."

## 24. The Last Meal

"It was said by the elders who convened the First Buddhist Council, 'When he had eaten Cunda the smith's food, thus have I heard, the Buddha felt a dire sickness, a sharp pain even unto death.'[3] Yet the Blessed One also said, 'These two offerings of food, Ānanda, are of equal merit and are much more effective than any others: that, after which the Tathāgata attains to supreme enlightenment; and that, after which the Tathāgata attains to *parinibbāna*'.[4]

---

[1] Jā. iii. 24, *see* quotations.

[2] Jā. iv. 210, *see* quotations.

[3] D. ii. 128, *see* quotations.

[4] D. ii. 135, *see* quotations.

"If severe pains fell upon him after taking that last meal then the latter statement must be wrong."

"The last offering of food is of great advantage because of the Tathāgata's attainment of *parinibbāna*. It was not because of the food that the sickness fell upon the Blessed One but because of the extreme weakness of his body and the proximity of his death. These two offerings of food were of great and incomparable merit because of the attainment of the nine successive absorptions in forward and reverse order, which the Tathāgata gained after partaking of that food."

## 25. *Adoration of Relics*

"The Blessed One said, 'Do not hinder yourselves, Ānanda, with honouring the remains of the Tathāgata[1] Yet on the other hand he said, 'Honour the relics of him who is worthy of honour, acting in that way you will go from this world to heaven.'[2] Which of these statements is right?"

"It was not to all men, O king, but to the sons of the conqueror [monks] that the first advice was given. Paying reverence to relics is not their work, but rather grasping the true nature of all formations, reasoning [paying attention to impermanence *etc*.], insight meditation, getting hold of the essence of the meditation object, devotion to their own spiritual welfare, that is the work of the monks. Just, O king, as it is the business of princes to learn the arts of warfare and the laws of property while husbandry, trading and care of cattle are the business of householders."

## 26. *The Buddha's Foot is Injured*

"You say that when the Blessed One walked along, the great earth, unconscious though it is, filled up the hollows and levelled the ground before his feet.[3] Yet you say that a splinter of rock grazed his foot.[4] Why then didn't that splinter of rock turn away from his foot?"

"O king, the splinter of rock did not fall by itself, but a rock was thrown down by Devadatta. Two rocks came together and intercepted it but a splinter of rock broke off and grazed the Blessed One's foot. A thing intercepted can easily slip through just as water taken up in the hands can easily slip through the fingers."

---

[1] D. ii. 141, *see* quotations.

[2] Vv. 75 v 8, *see* quotations.

[3] Untraced, but *cf.* DA. 45, *see* quotations.

[4] Vin. ii. 193, *see* quotations.

## 27. The True Recluse

"The Blessed One said, 'A man becomes a recluse by the destruction of the floods [sensuality, desire for rebirth, personality belief and ignorance].'[1] Yet he also said, 'He is known in the world as a recluse who has these four qualities: patience, moderation in food, relinquishment and being without possessions.'[2] Now these four qualities are also found in those who are still imperfect, in whom the defilements have not yet been totally rooted out. This too is a double-edged problem."

"Both these statements, O king, were made by the Blessed One but the first is an inclusive statement whereas the second was said of the characteristics of recluses in general."

## 28. The Boasting of the Buddha

"The Blessed One said, 'If anyone should speak in praise of me, my teaching or the Order you should not on account of that be elated.'[3] Yet he was so delighted when Sela the Brahman praised him that he magnified his own virtue and said, 'A king, Sela, am I, the king supreme of righteousness. The royal chariot wheel of righteousness do I set rolling on — the wheel that no one can ever turn back.'[4] This too is a double-edged problem."

"Both statements, O king, are correct but the first was made to set forth truthfully and exactly the real nature of the teaching. The second passage was not spoken for gain, fame, nor in a biased way, nor for the sake of winning over followers but was spoken with compassion and the knowledge that thereby three hundred brahmans would attain to knowledge of the truth."

## 29. Who Deserves Punishment?

"The Blessed One said, 'Doing no injury to anyone, dwell full of love and kindness in the world.'[5] Yet he also said, 'Restrain him who deserves restraint and encourage him who deserves encouragement.'[6] Now,

[1] A. ii. 238, Pug. 63, *see* quotations.

[2] Ku.5 p. 204 Jātaka, Burmese edition, *see* quotations.

[3] D. i. 3; *cf.* M. i. 140, *see* quotations.

[4] M. ii. Sta. 92; Sn. v 554, *see* quotations.

[5] Jā. iv. 71 v 9, *see* quotations.

[6] Jā. v. 116, *see* quotations.

restraint means the cutting off of hands and feet, imprisonment and so forth. If the first statement is correct then the second cannot be right."

"O king, to do no injury is a doctrine approved of by all the Buddhas; the second injunction however was used figuratively. It means restrain the agitated mind, encourage the slothful mind; restrain the unwholesome mind, encourage the wholesome mind; restrain unwise reflection, encourage wise reflection; restrain wrong practice, encourage right practice; the ignoble should be restrained, the noble encouraged; the thief [the evil-minded monk who desires gain, praise and fame] should be restrained and the honest man [the sincere monk who desires only to destroy defilements] should be encouraged."

"Now you have come round to the sense in my question. For how, venerable Nāgasena, is a robber to be subdued?"

"Thus, great king: if deserving rebuke let him be rebuked, if deserving a fine let him be fined, if deserving banishment let him be banished, if deserving death let him be put to death."

"Is then, Nāgasena, the execution of robbers part of the doctrine laid down by the Tathāgata?"

"Certainly not, O king. Whosoever may be put to death, he does not suffer execution by reason of the opinion put forward by the Tathāgata. He suffers by reason of what he himself has done."[1]

## *30. Dismissal of the Order*

"It was said by the Blessed One, 'I harbour not anger nor sulkiness'.[2] Yet he dismissed Sāriputta and Moggallāna with their disciples.[3] Was it then not in anger that he did this?"

"The Tathāgata did dismiss the monks but not in anger. It was due to what they themselves had done that they were dismissed. As the great earth does not feel anger if a man stumbles and falls. It is the man's own fault that he stumbles. So too the Blessed One does not feel ill-will of any kind. He sent them away knowing, 'It will be for their good, happiness, purification and deliverance from suffering'."

---

[1] Capital punishment was the norm and severe corporal punishment was also practised in the Buddha's time.

[2] Sn. v 19, *see* quotations.

[3] M. ii. Sta. 67.

# CHAPTER ELEVEN

## THE SOLVING OF DILEMMAS (Contd.)

### *31. The Murder of Moggallāna*

"This was said by the Blessed One, 'Moggallāna is the chief of those among my disciples who possess supernormal power.'[1] Yet he was beaten to death with clubs.[2] Why did his powers fail him?"

"That, O king, was because he was then overwhelmed by the greater power of *kamma*. Even among things that are beyond the scope of the imagination one may be more powerful than the others. Among things that are unimaginable *kamma* is the most powerful. It is precisely the effect of *kamma* that overcomes and rules the rest, for no other influence is of any avail to the man in whom *kamma* is working out its inevitable result. Just as a man who has been found guilty of a crime will be punished and there is nothing his relatives may do to prevent it."

### *32. Secrecy of the Vinaya*

"It was said by the Blessed One, 'The *Dhamma* and *Vinaya* proclaimed by the Tathāgata shine forth when they are displayed and not when they are unrevealed.'[3] So why is the recitation of the *Pātimokkha* done only in the presence of *bhikkhus*[4] and why is the *Vinaya Piṭaka* closed and privy to *bhikkhus?*"[5]

"O king, the reason for the *Pātimokkha* being open only to *bhikkhus* is that it is a custom of all previous Buddhas, secondly out of respect for the *Vinaya* and thirdly out of respect for the *bhikkhus*. Just, O king, as the traditions of warriors are handed down among warriors alone so it is the tradition of the Tathāgatas that the recitation of the *Pātimokkha* should take place only among *bhikkhus*. The *Vinaya* is venerable and profound. He who has reached proficiency in it may exhort others thus, 'Let not this profound teaching fall into the hands of those who are unwise where it would be despised and

---

[1] A. i. 23, *see* quotations.

[2] DhA. iii. 65f. Commentary on Dhp. vv 137 140.

[3] A. i. 283, *see* quotations.

[4] Vin. i. 115, 135, *see* quotations.

[5] There is no prohibition against teaching the *Vinaya* to lay people.

condemned, treated shamefully, ridiculed and found fault with'.[1] Just as there are priceless possessions of kings that should not be used by men of the world, so too, the training and traditions of the Blessed One for *bhikkhus* are their priceless possessions. That is why the recitation of the *Pātimokkha* takes place only among *bhikkhus.*"

## 33. Intentional Lying

"It has been said by the Blessed One, 'Intentional lying is an offence involving expulsion.'[2] Yet he also said, 'Intentional lying is a light offence that must be confessed to another *bhikkhu.*[3] How can both of these be right?"

"If a man were to strike another with his hand what punishment would you give him?"

"If the victim refused to overlook the matter we would fine the assailant."

"But if a man were to strike you, what punishment would you give him?"

"We would cut off his hands and feet, scalp him, plunder all his wealth and uproot his family up to the seventh generation."

"Just so, O king, the offence is light or heavy according to the subject matter. Intentional lying about the attainment of super-human states such as the absorptions, supernormal power or the paths of spiritual attainment is an offence involving expulsion. However, intentional lying about other matters is only an offence involving confession."

---

[1] T.W. Rhys Davids had this to say about esoteric Buddhism; "The fact is that there has never been any such thing as esoteric teaching in Buddhism, and that the modern so called esoteric Buddhism is neither esoteric nor Buddhism. Its tenets, so far as they are Indian at all, are perfectly accessible, are well known to all those who choose to study the books of Indian mysticism, and are Hindu, not Buddhist. They are, indeed, quite contradictory to Buddhism, of which the authors of what they ignorantly call Esoteric Buddhism know but very little — that little being only a portion of those beliefs which have been the common ground to all religious teachers in India. If one doctrine, more than any other, is distinctive of Buddhism, it is the ignoring, in ethics of the time-honoured belief in a soul — that is, in the old sense, in a separate creature inside the body, which flies out of it, like a bird out of a cage, when the body dies. Yet the Theosophists, who believe, I am told, in seven souls inside the human body (which would be worse according to true Buddhism than seven devils), still venture to call themselves Buddhists, and do not see the absurdity of their position!"

[2] Vin. iii. 94ff, *see* quotations.

[3] Vin. iii. 59, 66; Vin. iv. 2, *see* quotations.

## 34. *Investigations of the Bodhisatta*

"It was said by the Blessed One in the discourse on natural law, 'Long ago had the Bodhisatta's parents, chief disciples, *etc.*, been predestined for the Bodhisatta.'[1] Yet it was also said, 'While still in the Tusita heaven the Bodhisatta makes eight investigations: whether the right moment has come for him to be reborn, the continent, the country, the family, the mother, the time in the womb, the month of the birth, and the time of the going forth.'[2] If his parents were already predestined why was it necessary for him to consider these things?"

"Both these statements, O king, are correct. With respect to eight things the future should be investigated before it comes to pass. A merchant should inspect goods before he buys them, an elephant should try a path with his trunk before he treads it, a carter should survey a ford before he crosses it, a pilot should plumb a shore he has not seen before, a physician should assess the remaining life-span of a patient before treating him, a traveller should inspect a bridge before he walks on it, a *bhikkhu* should know the time before he starts his meal, and a Bodhisatta should investigate the family before he is born."

## 35. *On Suicide*

"It has been said by the Blessed One, 'A monk should not try to commit suicide [throw himself down from a precipice]; whoever does so should be dealt with according to the rule.'[3] Yet, on the other hand, you say that on whatever topic he was addressing the monks, he always, and with various similes, exhorted them to bring about the destruction of birth, old age, disease and death, and whosoever overcame them he honoured with high praise."

"O king, it is because an *arahant* is of great benefit to beings that he laid down that prohibition. One who has reached the goal is like a boat to carry people over the floods of sensuality, desire for rebirth, personality belief and ignorance; like a mighty rain-cloud he fills their minds with satisfaction and he is a guide to those who are lost. Out of compassion for living beings the Blessed One said, 'A monk is not to

---

[1] *Mahāpadhāna Sutta*, D. ii. 17-20, *see* quotations.

[2] Jā. i. 48; DA. 428, (only 5 mentioned), *see* quotations.

[3] Vin. iii. 74, 82 (an offence of wrong doing), *see* quotations.

commit suicide.' And what is the reason the Blessed One urged us to put an end to birth, old age and death? Because of the limitless nature of the suffering of the round of rebirths the Blessed One, out of compassion for beings, urged them in many ways, with various similes to free themselves from the round of rebirths."

## 36. *Protection by Loving-kindness*

"It has been said by the Blessed One, 'These eleven advantages may be expected by one who practises and makes a habit of loving-kindness towards all beings: he sleeps in peace; he wakes in peace; he dreams no evil dreams; he becomes dear to human beings and to non-human beings; the gods protect him; neither fire, nor poison, nor weapons can harm him; his mind is quickly concentrated; his countenance is serene; he dies unconfused; and if he attains no higher he is reborn in the Brahmā realm.'[1] Why then was the youth Sāma, who dwelt full of loving-kindness, hit by a poisoned arrow fired by King Piliyakkha?"[2]

"O king, these eleven virtues of loving-kindness are dependent on love itself and not on the character of the person who practises it. Sāma practised the meditation on loving-kindness all the time. However, while he was collecting water, his mind lapsed from the meditation and at that moment King Piliyakkha shot him, so the arrow was able to hurt him."

## 37. *Why Did Devadatta Prosper?*

"Although you say that good deeds lead to rebirth in heaven or fortunate human births and that evil deeds lead to rebirth in states of misery or unfortunate human births; Devadatta, who was full of evil qualities, was often born in a position of superiority over the Bodhisatta,[3] who was full of good qualities. Thus Nāgasena, when Devadatta became the family chaplain of Brahmadatta the king of Benares, then the Bodhisatta was a wretched outcaste. This is one case in which the Bodhisatta was inferior to Devadatta in birth and reputation. Again, when Devadatta became a king, a mighty monarch of the earth, the Bodhisatta was an elephant. In that case too, the Bodhisatta was inferior to Devadatta; and in many other cases too."

"It was as you say, O king."

---

[1] A. v. 342, Jā. ii. 61; Vism. 311f, *see* quotations.

[2] Jā. vi. 76, *see* quotations.

[3] *cf.* Jā. Nos. 72, 122, 222, 241, 313, 358, 422, 438, 472, 474, 482, 492, 514, 516, 518.

"Then it follows that good and evil bear equal fruit."

"Nay, not so, O king. Devadatta was opposed by everybody but no one was hostile to the Bodhisatta. Yet, when he was a king, Devadatta protected and served the people and gave gifts to recluses and brahmans according to his inclination. Of no one can it be said, O king, that without generosity, self-restraint, observance of precepts and other virtues, that he can reach prosperity. Nevertheless, all beings who are swept along in the endless round of rebirths meet with pleasant and unpleasant companions just as water whirled along in a river meets with pure and impure things. However, the comparison between the Bodhisatta and Devadatta should be regarded in the light of the unimaginable length of the round of rebirths; and it should also be remembered that the Bodhisatta was in heaven for aeons while Devadatta boiled in hell."

## 38. *The Weakness of Women*

"It is said that a woman will always commit adultery if she finds a suitable lover.[1] Yet Mahāsodha's wife refused to do any wrong even though offered a thousand pieces of gold."[2]

"Amaradevī was virtuous. Through fear of censure in this world and through the fear of suffering in purgatory and because she loved her husband, and despised immorality and treasured virtue — for all of these reasons the opportunity seemed not fit to her. Her husband, Mahāsodha, was an ideal man so she found no other man comparable to him; so for this reason too, she did no wrong."

## 39. *Ānanda's Courage*

"It was said by the Blessed One that *arahants* have laid aside all fear.[3] Yet when the intoxicated elephant Dhanapālaka was charging towards the Buddha five hundred *arahants* fled, leaving Ānanda alone to protect the Buddha.[4] If *arahants* are free from all fear why did they flee?"

---

[1] Jā. v. 435. One should not overlook the fact that if a woman does commit adultery, at least one man is usually involved too. So one should not infer that men are any more virtuous than women.

[2] Jā. vi. 367, *see* quotations.

[3] Dhp. v 351; Sn. 621, *see* quotations.

[4] Vin. ii. 194; Jā. v. 33ff, *see* quotations. The ferocious elephant was known as Nāḷāgiri but after he was tamed by the Buddha's *mettā* he bowed down and worshipped him. The crowd were thrilled to see this transformation and heaped ornaments upon the elephant's back. Henceforth he was known as Dhanapālaka, bearer of wealth.

"They did not flee because of fear, O king, the *arahants* are free from fear. They only moved aside so Ānanda's devotion to the Buddha would be manifested. They realised that if they didn't move the elephant wouldn't be able to approach. Ānanda, who was not yet an *arahant,* remained by the Buddha's side to protect him and thus his courage and devotion were displayed. Because of this event great masses of people were emancipated from the bondage of defilements. It was because they foresaw these advantages that they moved aside."

## 40. *The Buddha's Change of Heart*

"You say that the Buddha is omniscient yet when the company of monks led by Sāriputta and Moggallāna had been dismissed by him the Sakyans of Cātumā and Brahmā Sahampati placated the Buddha with similes.[1] Did he then not know those similes? If he did then why did he need to be placated?"

"The Tathāgata, O king, was omniscient yet he was conciliated by those similes. It was by means of similes that he himself had first preached that he was conciliated, and it was being thus won over that he signified his approval. It was, O king, as when an attendant novice serves his teacher with almsfood brought by the teacher himself and thereby pleases him and wins him over."

[1] M. ii. Sta. 67, *see* quotations.

# CHAPTER TWELVE

## THE SOLVING OF DILEMMAS (Contd.)

### *41. On Dwelling Places*

"It was said by the Blessed One:

"Fear is born from intimacy,
Dust is from a house arisen.
Homeless, free from intimacy,
This is the sage's vision."[1]

"Yet he also said:

"Let the wise man have dwellings built
and lodge learned men therein."[2]

"If the former statement was made by the Blessed One then the latter must be wrong."

"Both statements were made by the Tathāgata, O king, but the first was an inclusive statement as to the nature of things and as to what it is proper for recluses to desire. However, the second statement was said concerning two matters only. The gift of a dwelling place has been highly praised by the Buddhas because those who have made such a gift will be delivered from birth, old age, disease and death. Secondly, if there is a dwelling place it is easy for those who wish to listen to the Dhamma to visit the *bhikkhus,* whereas if they stayed in the forest it would not be. However, it does not follow that the *bhikkhus* have a longing for a dwelling place."

### *42. Restraint of the Stomach*

"The Blessed One said, 'Do not be heedless in standing for alms, be restrained regarding the stomach.'[3] However, he also said, 'There were times, Udāyi, when I ate a full bowl of food or even more.'[4] This too is a double-edged problem."

---

[1] Sn. v 207, *see* quotations.

[2] Vin. ii. 147; S. i. 100, *see* quotations.

[3] Dhp. v 168. When the Buddha returned to his birth place he went for alms since his relatives had not yet invited him for the meal. *See* quotations.

[4] M. ii. 7, *see* quotations.

"Both statements are correct, O king, but the former statement is inclusive and cannot be proved wrong. He who has no restraint as regards the stomach will kill living beings or steal for the sake of his stomach. It was bearing this in mind that the Blessed One said, 'Do not be heedless in standing for alms, be restrained regarding the stomach.' He who has self-control gains a clear insight into the Four Noble Truths and fulfils the life of a recluse. Didn't a mere parrot, O king, by his restraint as to his stomach shake the heaven of the thirty-three and bring down Sakka to wait on him?[1] However, when the Blessed One said, 'There were times, Udāyi, when I ate a full bowl of food or even more' it was concerning himself. He had accomplished all that can be accomplished by restraint, and like a perfect gem that needs no more polishing, he needed no more training."

## *43. The Best of Men*

"The Blessed One said, 'I, monks, am a Brahman, one to ask a favour of, always ready to give; this body that I bear will be my last, I am the supreme healer and physician.'[2] Yet on the other hand he said, 'The chief among my disciples as regards physical health is Bakkula.'[3] Now it is well known that the Blessed One suffered several times from diseases whereas Bakkula was always healthy. If the first statement is true then why was the Buddha less healthy than Bakkula?"

"Although it is true that Bakkula surpassed the Buddha in the matter of health and other disciples also surpassed him in other aspects yet the Blessed One surpassed them all in respect of virtue, concentration and wisdom; and it was in reference to this that he spoke the verse, 'I, monks, am a Brahman, one to ask a favour of, always ready to give; this body that I bear will be my last, I am the supreme healer and physician'."

"The Blessed One, O king, whether he is sick or not; whether he is practising the ascetic practices or not — there is no other being comparable to him. For this, O king, was said in the *Saṃyutta Nikāya,* 'Just as, monks, of all creatures; whether footless, or having two, four or many feet; whether having form or formless; whether conscious or unconscious, or

---

[1] Jā. No. 429.

[2] Iti. 101, *see* quotations.

[3] As a result of treating Buddhas Anomadassī and Vipassī. A. i. 24, *see* quotations.

neither conscious nor unconscious — of these the Tathāgata, the *arahant*, the Fully Enlightened One, is reckoned as the chief...'."[1]

## 44. The Ancient Path

"It was said by the Blessed One, 'The Tathāgata is the discoverer of a way that was unknown.'[2] Yet he also said, 'Now I perceived, O monks, the ancient path along which the previous Buddhas walked.'[3] This too is a double-edged problem."

"It was because the path shown by previous Buddhas had long since disappeared and was not known by anyone, man or god, that the Buddha said, 'The Tathāgata is the discoverer of a way that was unknown.' Though that way had disintegrated, become impassable and lost to view — the Tathāgata, having gained a thorough knowledge of it, saw by his eye of wisdom that it was the path used by previous Buddhas. Therefore he said; 'Now I perceived, O monks, the ancient path along which the previous Buddhas walked.' It is as when a man clears the jungle and sets free a piece of land it is called his land though he did not make the land."

## 45. The Bodhisatta's Weakness

"It was said by the Blessed One, 'Already in former births when I was a man I had acquired the habit of not inflicting harm on living beings.'[4] However, when he was an ascetic called Lomasa Kassapa he had hundreds of animals killed and offered as a sacrifice.[5] Why was he not compassionate then?"

"That sacrifice, O king, was done when Lomasa Kassapa was out of his mind through infatuation with Princess Candavatī; not when he was conscious of what he was doing. Just as a madman, when out of his senses, will step into a fire or catch hold of a venomous snake or run naked through the streets, so it was only because the Bodhisatta was out of his mind that he performed the great sacrifice. Now an evil

---

[1] S. v. 41.

[2] S. iii. 66; *cf.* S. i. 190, *see* quotations.

[3] *i.e.* The Path leading to *nibbāna*. S. ii. 105, *see* quotations.

[4] D. iii. 166, *see* quotations.

[5] Jā. iii. 30ff, 514ff, *see* quotations. In the *Jātaka* story, Kassapa ordered the animals brought for slaughter but when they were all tied down at the stake he came to his senses and set them free.

act done by a madman is not considered a grievous offence, nor is it grievous in respect of the fruit that it brings in a future life. Suppose, O king, that a madman had been guilty of a capital offence, what punishment would you inflict upon him?"

"What punishment is due to a madman? We should order him to be beaten and set free, that is all."

"So then, O king, it follows that the offence of one who is mad is pardonable.[1] Just so was it in the case of Lomasa Kassapa who, after he regained his senses, renounced the world and became assured of rebirth in the Brahmā realm."

## 46. *Respect for the Robe*

"Even when the Bodhisatta was an elephant he had respect for the yellow robe[2] but you also say that when he was the Brahman youth Jotipāla, even though he was then endowed with the discernment of a human being, he reviled and abused the Buddha Kassapa, calling him a shaveling and good-for-nothing monk.[3] How can both of these statements be true?"

"O king, the Bodhisatta's rudeness when he was the Brahman youth Jotipāla was due to his birth and upbringing; all his family were unbelievers who worshipped Brahmā and thought that Brahmans were the highest among men. Just, O king, as even the coolest water will become warm when in contact with fire so, Jotipāla, though he was full of merit, yet when he was reborn into a family of unbelievers he became as if blind and reviled the Tathāgata. However, when he went to the presence of the Buddha Kassapa he realised his virtue and became his devoted disciple."

## 47. *The Merit of the Potter*

"It was said by the Blessed One, 'For three whole months the dwelling place of Ghatīkāra the potter remained open to the sky but no rain fell on it.'[4] Yet it was said that rain fell on the hut of Buddha

---

[1] *cf.* Vin. iii. 32, where there is no offence for one who is mad.

[2] Jā. v. 49, *see* quotations.

[3] M. ii. 47, Sta. 81, *see* quotations.

[4] M. ii. 53, *see* quotations.

Kassapa.[1] Why did the hut of the Tathāgata get wet? If rain fell on the hut of the Buddha who had so much merit then it must be false that no rain fell on the hut of Ghatīkāra because of his great merit."

"O king, Ghatīkāra was a good man, full of virtue and rich in merit, who supported his blind parents by his humble trade. While he was away from the house, the monks, having confidence in the unstinting generosity of Ghatīkāra, took away some thatch from the roof of his house to repair the hut of Buddha Kassapa. When Ghatīkāra returned he was neither angry nor disappointed but was full of joy because he had gained so much merit by giving something to the Tathāgata and ecstatic at the thought, 'The Blessed One has full confidence in me.' So great was his merit that it brought forth its result in this very life. The Tathāgata on the other hand, was not short of merit because the rain fell on his hut but he had considered, 'Let people not find fault saying that the Buddhas gain a livelihood by the use of supernormal powers.' Therefore the rain fell on his hut as it did on all the others except that of Ghatīkāra."

## *48. King or Brahman?*

"The Blessed One said, 'I, monks, am a Brahman, one to ask a favour of.'[2] However, he also said, 'A king, Sela, am I.'[3] If, Nāgasena, he was a king, then he must have spoken falsely when he said he was a Brahman, for he must have been either a Khattiya (a warrior) or a Brahman, he could not have belonged to both castes."

"It was not on account of his birth that he called himself a Brahman but because he was free from defilements, had attained to the certainty of knowledge and because he was one who maintained the ancient traditions of teaching and learning by heart, self-control and discipline.[4] As a king rules the people with the law, the Buddha rules the people by teaching Dhamma; bringing joy to those who live rightly and reproving those who transgress the noble law. Like a king who rules justly rules for a long time, the Buddha's religion endures for a long time because of his special qualities of righteousness."

---

[1] M. ii. 54, *see* quotations.

[2] Iti. 101.

[3] Sn. v 554.

[4] *See* Dhp. Brāhmaṇavagga.

## *49. Right Livelihood*

"You say that the Blessed One did not accept alms received by chanting verses[1] but when preaching to laymen he generally spoke first of the benefits of giving and accepted the gifts offered.[2] If the first is true then why did he accept gifts gained by preaching?"

"It is the custom of the Tathāgatas to preach first of the benefits of giving to soften men's hearts before going on to preach of morality and higher matters but not on account of that could they justly be accused of hinting to get gifts. There is hinting that is improper and there is hinting that is blameless. Herein, if a *bhikkhu* begs for alms standing in an inconvenient place or making signs this is improper hinting;[3] but if he stands in the proper place where there are people who want to give and moves on if they do not want to give then this is proper and does not amount to hinting. That meal of the ploughman was offered in order to refute the subject of the verse recited therefore the Tathāgata rejected it."

## *50. The Reluctance of the Buddha*

"You say that for four aeons and 100,000 world cycles the Bodhisatta practised the perfections in order to gain omniscience[4] yet after he had gained omniscience his mind inclined to not teaching the Dhamma.[5] Like an archer who had practised for many days might hesitate when the day for battle had come, even so did the Blessed One hesitate to teach the Dhamma. Was it then because of fear, or lack of clarity, or weakness, or because he was not omniscient that he hesitated?"

"No, great king, it was for none of those reasons. It was due to the profound nature of the Dhamma and to the exceedingly strong passion and delusion of beings that the Blessed One hesitated and considered to whom he should teach it and in what manner so that they would understand. Just, O king, as a king when he calls to mind the many people who gain their livelihood in dependence on him — the body-guards, courtiers, merchants, soldiers, messengers, ministers

---

[1] S. i. 167, Sn. v 81, *see* quotations.

[2] *cf.* D. i. Sta. 5.

[3] Vism. 28.

[4] *Cf.* Cp. i. 1, *see* quotations.

[5] Vin. i. 5; *cf.* S. i. 136, *see* quotations.

and nobles — he might be exercised at the thought; 'How can I conciliate them all?' Just so, O king, when the Tathāgata called to mind the strong passion and delusion of beings that he inclined rather to inaction than to preaching. It is also in the natural order of things that the Buddha should teach the Dhamma at the request of Brahmā, for at that time all men were worshippers of Brahmā and placed their reliance on him. Therefore if one so high and mighty as Brahmā should incline to hearing Dhamma then the whole world of gods and men would become inclined to it and so for that reason too the Buddha waited to be asked before preaching the Dhamma."

## 51. *The Buddha's Teachers*

"The Blessed One said, 'I have no teacher, one like me does not exist. In the world with its gods no one equals me.'[1] Again he said, 'In this way, monks, did Āḷāra the Kālāma, being my teacher, set me, his pupil, on exactly the same level as himself and honour me with the highest honour.'[2] This too is a double-edged problem."

"O king, when the Blessed One spoke of Āḷāra the Kālāma as his teacher he referred to the time when he was still a Bodhisatta and before he had attained Buddhahood. He was merely a teacher of worldly wisdom. It was in regard to transcendental matters such as knowledge of the Four Noble Truths and *nibbāna* that he said, 'I have no teacher, one like me does not exist. In the world with its gods no one equals me'."

---

[1] Vin. i. 8; M. i. 171, *see* quotations.

[2] M. i. 165, *see* quotations.

# CHAPTER THIRTEEN

## THE SOLVING OF DILEMMAS (Contd.)

### 52. *Two Buddhas Cannot Exist Together*

"The Blessed One said, 'It is impossible that in one world two Perfectly Enlightened Buddhas could exist at the same time.'[1] Yet, Nāgasena, if all the Tathāgatas teach the same teaching why shouldn't they exist together? If there were two they could teach at ease and the world would be even more illumined."

"O king, if two Buddhas were to exist simultaneously this great earth could not bear the weight of their combined goodness, it would tremble and shake and break up.[2] Suppose, O king, a man had eaten as much food as he wanted so that he had no room for any more. Then if he were to eat the same amount of food again would he be at ease?"

"Certainly not, venerable sir, if he were to eat again he would die."

"Likewise, O king, this earth could no more bear a second Tathāgata than that man could bear a second meal. Also, if there were two Buddhas, disputes would arise between their disciples and, moreover, the statement that says the Buddha is supreme and has no equal would become false."

"Well has this dilemma been explained. Even an unintelligent man would be satisfied how much more a wise one.[3] Well said, Nāgasena, I accept it as you say."

### 53. *Gifts to the Order*

"When Mahāpajāpatī Gotamī offered a bathing robe[4] to the Buddha he told her, 'Give it to the Order Gotamī. If you give it to the Order I will be honoured and the Order too.' Was it because the Order is more important than the Buddha?"

---

[1] M. iii. 65; A. i. 27; Vbh. 336, *see* quotations.

[2] At the birth of the Bodhisatta the earth shook seven times.

[3] Both Rhys Davids and I.B. Horner have translated the Pali: *kiṃ pana mādiso mahāpañño.* "...how much more then a wise man like me." This makes Milinda seem conceited and I can't see any reason for translating the passage like that.

[4] *Vassikasātikaṃ. See Pācittiya* 91.

"O king it was not because an offering to him would not bear great fruit, but in order to show the greatness of the Order so that in times to come the Order might be esteemed. As sir, a father praises his son in the royal court thinking, 'If he is established here now, he will be honoured by the people after I am gone'. Or suppose, O king, some man should bring a present to a king and the king presented that gift to someone else — to a soldier or a messenger — would that man therefore become superior to the king?"

"Certainly not, venerable sir. That man receives his wages from the king and it was the king who placed him in that position."

"Just so, O king, the Order did not become superior to the Tathāgata merely by the fact of a gift. There is not, O king, any being more worthy of gifts than the Tathāgata[1] for this was said by the Blessed One himself:

> "There is one being; monks, who is born into the world for the good and benefit of many, out of compassion for the world, for the advantage and benefit of gods and men. Who is that being? A Tathāgata, an *arahant,* Buddha supreme."[2]

## 54. *The Advantages of a Recluse's Life*

"The Blessed One said, 'I would praise either a layman or a monk who has practised rightly and attained the right method.'[3] If a layman, enjoying the pleasures of the senses, dwelling with wife and children, and using scents and accepting gold and silver can attain *arahantship* what is the advantage of being a monk with a shaven head, dependent on alms, fulfilling one hundred and fifty precepts[4] and adopting the thirteen ascetic practices? Your austerity is without effect, your renunciation is useless, your observance of the precepts is barren, your taking of the extra vows is vain. What is the use of heaping up hardship for yourselves if bliss can be reached in comfort?"

---

[1] The author seems to have missed the point here. *cf.* M. iii. 256: "But when I, Ānanda, say that an offering to the Order is incalculable and immeasurable I by no means say that a gift graded as to individuals is of greater fruit than an offering to the Order."

[2] A. i. 20, *see* quotations.

[3] M. ii. 197, A. i. 69, *see* quotations.

[4] Excluding the 75 training rules there are 152.

"It is true what you say that the one who is practising rightly is best whether he is a monk or a layman. If a recluse, thinking 'I am a recluse' does not practice rightly then he is far from recluseship. How much more then a householder in a layman's clothes! Nevertheless, the benefit of being a recluse is too great to measure. Being of few desires he is easily contented, he is aloof from society, strenuous, homeless, he fulfils the precepts, he is austere and skilled in the practice of shaking off defilements. That is why he can quickly accomplish any task that he undertakes; just, O king, as your javelin, because it is smooth and straight, can quickly reach its target."

## 55. The Practice of Austerities

"When the Bodhisatta was practising austerity with the utmost exertion he did not reach his goal so he abandoned that practice thinking, 'Might there not be some other way to liberation?'[1] Yet when instructing his disciples he said:

> "Bestir yourselves, renounce,
> Exert yourselves in my teaching,
> And destroy death's army
> As an elephant a house of reeds."[2]

"Why then did the Tathāgata instruct his disciples to follow a course that he himself had abandoned?"

"Because then, O king, and still now too, that is the only path and it is along that path that the Bodhisatta attained Buddhahood. Although the Bodhisatta, exerting himself strenuously, reduced the food he was taking to nothing at all, and by that lack of food became weak, yet when he returned to the use of solid food, it was by exertion that he attained Buddhahood. There was no fault in exertion itself but it was due only to the lack of food that exertion failed to bring its result. If a man, through too much haste, were to become exhausted and fall down unable to go on, it would not be the fault of the earth that he fell down but due to his excessive exertion. If a man were to wear a robe and never have it washed, the fault would not lie with the water but

---

[1] M. i. 246, *see* quotations.

[2] S. i. 156, Kvu. 203, Thag 256, *see* quotations.

with the man. That is why the Tathāgata exhorted and led his disciples along that very path; for that path is always ready, and always right."

## 56. *Reverting to Laylife*

"Is it right to admit laymen to the Order before they have attained to the path of stream-entry? If such men give up the monk's life people might think that the religion is fruitless."

"If, O king, there was a pond of pure water and a man in need of a bath went there but turned back without bathing would the people blame the man or the pond?"

"They would blame the man."

"Even so, O king, the Tathāgata has constructed the pond full of the pure Dhamma thinking, 'Those who have defilements but are intelligent can remove their defilements here.' However, if anyone should revert to the household life without having removed his defilements then the people would blame him, there would be no reason to find fault with the teaching. If only stream-winners were allowed to go forth then going forth would not be for the sake of purification. If a man, having had a bathing pond dug, said, 'Let only those who have already bathed make use of it' would that be of any use? Moreover, those who revert to the household life thereby show up five special qualities of the conqueror's teaching. They show how glorious it is, how pure it is, how free from association with evil, how difficult it is to penetrate the Dhamma and how many are the restraints of the holy life.

"How do they show its glory? Just, O king, as a man of low birth, poor and unintelligent, who comes into possession of a mighty kingdom, will soon be overthrown and deprived of his glory. So too, those who are without wisdom and have little merit, when they renounce the world, are unable to carry out the teaching of the Conqueror and revert to the lower state.

"How do they show its purity? Just, O king, as water, when it falls onto a lotus, slips off and cannot adhere to it; so too, those who are impure by nature, crafty and holders of wrong views; when they have been admitted to the religion of the Conqueror, it is not long before they disperse from that pure and faultless religion, unable to adhere to it.

"How do they show its freedom from association with evil? Just as the ocean does not tolerate the presence of a corpse but quickly brings it ashore and casts it on dry land; so too, O king, those who are evil-minded and lazy are unable to remain in the Order in association with the *arahants* who are free from stains.

"How do they show how hard the Dhamma is to penetrate? Just, O king, as those archers who are clumsy and unskilled are unable to perform feats of archery like hair-splitting but miss the target; so too, those who are dull and stupid and renounce the world are unable to grasp the Four Noble Truths of the Conquerors, which are extremely subtle, and missing them, turn back to the lower state.

"How do they show the manifold restraints of the holy life? Just, O king, as a coward when he has gone to a battle and is surrounded by the forces of the enemy on all sides will turn back and take flight for fear of his life; so too, whoever are unrestrained, shameless, impatient and fickle, when they renounce the world they are unable to carry out the manifold precepts and revert to the lower state."

## 57. *The Mastery of the Arahants*

"You say that the *arahant* feels only one kind of feeling; physical feeling but not mental feeling.[1] How can this be so? The *arahant* keeps going by means of his body. Has he then no power over his body? Even a bird is the ruler over the nest in which it dwells."

"O king, there are ten conditions inherent in the body over which the *arahant* has no control: cold, heat, hunger, thirst, excrement, urine, fatigue, old age, disease and death. Just as all beings living on the great earth depend on it but have no control over it, so the *arahant* depends on his body but has no control over it."

"Why, Nāgasena, does the ordinary man feel both bodily and mental feeling?"

"Because of the untrained state of his mind. Like a hungry ox tied up by a weak grass rope would easily break free, so an ordinary man's mind becomes agitated by pain so he feels mental pain too. However, the *arahant's* mind is well trained, so when his body is affected by pain he fixes his mind firmly on the idea of impermanence. His mind is not agitated and he feels no mental pain, just as the trunk of a great tree is unmoved by the wind although its branches may sway."

---

[1] Untraced, *see* quotations.

## 58. *Heinous Crimes*

"If a layman had committed a heinous crime[1] before he entered the Order but was unaware of it would he be able to attain the path of a stream-winner?"

"No, he would not, because the basis for understanding the Dhamma has been destroyed in him."

"But you say that to him who is aware of an offence there comes remorse, which causes an obstruction in the mind, and so he cannot comprehend the truth.[2] Yet in him who is unaware of his offence there is no remorse and he remains with peace of mind."

"If, O king, a man had eaten poison but was not aware of it, would he still die?"

"Yes, venerable sir."

"Just so, O king, even though a man was not aware of his offence he would not be able to comprehend the truth."

"Surely, Nāgasena, this must be the word of the Conqueror and to look for any fault in it is vain. It must be as you say; and I accept it thus."

## 59. *The Unvirtuous*

"What is the difference between a layman who has done wrong and a monk who has done wrong?"

"There are ten qualities that distinguish a monk of poor moral habit from a layman of poor moral habit: he is full of reverence for the Buddha, Dhamma and Saṅgha; he recites the scriptures and asks about the meaning, he has heard much, he enters an assembly with dignity because he fears reproach, he guards himself in body and speech, he sets his mind on exertion, he is in company with the monks, and if he does any wrong he is discreet. Furthermore, in ten ways he purifies gifts of faith. By wearing the robe of the Buddhas, by his shaven head he bears the mark of sages, by being in company with

---

[1] The Pali has *Pārājikā* (offence of defeat) but a layman cannot commit these offences. What is meant is: killing one's mother, one's father, an *arahant*, drawing blood from a Tathāgata or violating a nun (the Sinhalese also gives damaging a bodhi tree). One guilty of these offences should not be ordained. If they are ordained they should be expelled.

[2] *cf.* A. iii. 165, "One who does amiss is dejected and knows not the mind's release." *See* quotations.

other monks, by his having taken refuge in the Buddha, Dhamma and Saṅgha, by his dwelling in a lonely place suitable for exertion, by his quest for the wealth of the Dhamma, by preaching the excellent Dhamma, because he takes the Dhamma as his guiding light, because he regards the Buddha as supreme, and by his observance of the *Uposatha*.[1] For all these reasons he is worthy of offerings even though he has fallen from virtue. Just as hot water extinguishes a fire, a monk of poor moral habit purifies the gift of benefactors, for this was said by the Tathāgata in the *Majjhima Nikāya*:

> "Whoever is virtuous and gives to the unvirtuous,
> A gift rightfully acquired, The mind well pleased,
> Firmly believing in the rich fruit of *kamma,*
> This is an offering purified by the giver."[2]

"Wonderful, Nāgasena, though I asked you an ordinary question you have given me an extraordinary answer, as a skilled cook would take an ordinary piece of meat and make with it a meal fit for a king."

## 60. *Is Water Alive?*

"There are some followers of other sects who say that you harm life by making use of cold water.[3] When water is heated in a vessel it makes various sounds; is this because it has a soul and is alive?"

"No great king, it is not alive. Water that is lying in shallow pools gets dried up by the heat of the sun and wind but it does not make any sound. Drums make a sound but they do not contain any life or living principle."

---

[1] The full moon and new moon days on which the monks recite the disciplinary rules.

[2] M. iii. Sta. 142, *see* quotations.

[3] *cf.* MLS. ii. 41 n 4; D. i. 167.

# CHAPTER FOURTEEN

## THE SOLVING OF DILEMMAS (Contd.)

### 61. *Be Without Impediments*

"The Blessed One said, 'Live devoted to and delighting in that which is without impediments.'[1] What is it that is without impediments?"

"The four fruits of the path and *nibbāna* are without impediments."

"But, Nāgasena, if that is so why do the monks concern themselves with learning the Buddha's discourses and with building repairs and offerings to the Order?"

"Those monks who do these things need to free their minds from impediments before they can attain the four fruits but those who are pure by nature have done such preparatory work in former births and can easily attain the fruits without such preparations. Just as in some areas a farmer can successfully grow crops without a fence but elsewhere he must first build a fence or a wall before he can grow a crop; or as one with supernormal powers can easily pick the fruits at the top of a tall tree but others have to construct a ladder first. Likewise, learning, enquiry, and other works are like a ladder and are helpful to those monks to reach the fruits of the four attainments. So long as there is need of discipleship when even those like Venerable Sāriputta find it impossible to attain *arahantship* without a teacher so there will be a use for recitation of the scriptures and thus will those disciples become free from obstructions and attain *arahantship.*"

### 62. *The Lay Arahant*

"You say that if a layman attains *arahantship* he must either enter the Order that very day or die and attain *parinibbāna*[2] Yet if he is unable to find a robe and bowl and preceptor then that exalted condition of *arahantship* is a waste for destruction of life is involved in it."

"The fault does not lie with *arahantship* but with the state of a layman because it is too weak to support *arahantship.* Just as, O king, although food protects the life of beings it will take away the life of one

---

[1] Untraced, but *cf.* M. i. 65. *See also* quotations.

[2] Untraced, but a layman can attain *arahantship. See* quotations.

whose digestion is weak — so too, if a layman attains *arahantship* he must, because of the weakness of that condition, enter the Order that very day or die."

## 63. The Offences of Arahants

"You say that an *arahant* cannot be of confused mindfulness.[1] Can he then commit any offence?"

"He can O king, as regards the size of his hut, by acting as a go-between, eating at the wrong time, eating what is not offered or in thinking he has not been invited when he has."

"But you say that those who fall into an offence do so either from ignorance or disrespect. If an *arahant* can fall into an offence and there is no disrespect in an *arahant* then is there confusion of mindfulness?"

"No there is no confusion of mindfulness in an *arahant*. There are two kinds of offence. There are those things that are blameworthy in the eyes of the world such as killing, stealing, *etc*., and there are those things that are only blameworthy for a monk such as eating at the wrong time, damaging trees and plants or playing in the water, and many other things of a similar kind. These things, O king, are not wrong in the eyes of the world but they are wrong for a monk. An *arahant* is incapable of transgressing the former type of precept but he may break the other kind because he doesn't know everything. He may not know the time of day or the name and clan of some woman but every *arahant* knows about freedom from suffering."

## 64. What is Not Found in the World

"There are many different things found in the world, Nāgasena, but tell me what is not to be found in the world."

"There are three things, O king, that are not to be found in the world: anything, either conscious or unconscious, that does not decay and perish, that formation *(saṅkhāra)* or conditioned thing that is permanent, and in the ultimate sense there is no such thing as a being."[2]

---

[1] *cf.* Pts. contr. 114, *see* quotations.

[2] Untraced. *See* quotations.

## 65. *The Uncaused*

"Nāgasena, there are things in the world that have come into existence through *kamma,* others are the result of a cause, and others are produced by season. Tell me, is there anything that does not fall into either of these three categories?"

"There are two such things, O king; space and *nibbāna.*"[1]

"Do not, Venerable Nāgasena, corrupt the words of the Conqueror, or answer a question without knowing what you are saying!"

"What have I said, O king, that you speak to me thus?"

"Venerable sir, it is right what you say about space but with hundreds of reasons did the Blessed One proclaim to his disciples the way to the realisation of *nibbāna* and yet you say that *nibbāna* is not the result of any cause."

"It is true, O king, that in many ways did the Blessed One point out a way to the realisation of *nibbāna* but he did not point out a cause for the arising of *nibbāna.*"

"Here, Nāgasena, we go from darkness to greater darkness; from uncertainty to utter confusion. If there is a father of a child we would expect to find a father of the father. Just so, if there is a cause for the realisation of *nibbāna* we would expect to find a cause for its arising."

"*Nibbāna,* O king, is unconstructed, therefore no cause has been pointed out for its production. It cannot be said of *nibbāna* that it has arisen or can arise; that it is past, present or future; or cognizable by the eye, ear, nose, tongue or body."

"Then, Nāgasena, *nibbāna* is a condition that does not exist!"

"*Nibbāna* does exist, O king, and can be cognized by the mind. A noble disciple whose mind is pure, lofty, sincere, unobstructed and free from craving can attain *nibbāna.*"

"Then explain by means of similes what *nibbāna* is."

"Is there such a thing as the wind?"

"Yes there is."

"Then explain by means of similes what the wind is."

"It is not possible to explain what the wind is by means of similes but it exists all the same."

"Just so, O king, *nibbāna* exists but it is impossible to describe."

---

[1] *See* quotations.

## *66. Modes of Production*

"What is it that is *kamma*-born, what cause-born, and what season-born? What is it that is none of these?"

"All beings, O king are *kamma*-born. Fire, and all things growing out of seeds are cause-born. The earth, water and wind are season-born. Space and *nibbāna* exist independently of *kamma,* cause and season. Of *nibbāna,* O king, it cannot be said that it is perceptible by the five senses, but it is perceptible by the mind. The disciple whose mind is pure, and free from obstructions can perceive *nibbāna*"

## *67. Demons*

"Are there such things as *yakkhas* (demons) in the world?"

"Yes, O king, there are."

"Then why aren't the remains of dead *yakkhas* seen?"

"Their remains are to be seen in the form of insects, such as maggots, ants, moths, snakes, scorpions, centipedes and other wild creatures."

"Who else, Nāgasena, could have solved this puzzle except one as wise as you!"

## *68. Laying Down of Rules for Monks*

"Those who are famous doctors are able to prescribe suitable medicine for a disease before the disease has arisen even though they are not omniscient. Why then, did the Tathāgata not lay down the rules for monks before the occasion arose but only when an offence had been committed and a great hue and cry was heard."

"The Tathāgata, O king, knew beforehand that all one hundred and fifty[1] rules would have to be laid down but he thought, 'If I lay down all of these rules at once there will be those who will not enter the Order for fear of the many regulations to be observed, therefore I will lay down the rules as the need arises'."[2]

---

[1] Mentioned also in Dilemma 54. Perhaps 150 rules were referred to as the 75 training rules are common to novices as well and hence there were 152 rules exclusively for monks.

[2] *cf.* Vin. iii. 9, 10.

## 69. *The Heat of the Sun*

"Why is the heat of the sun sometimes fierce and sometimes not?"

"Obscured by four things, O king, the sun does not shine fiercely; by storm clouds, by mist, by dust clouds, or by the moon."[1]

"It is remarkable, Nāgasena, that the glorious sun, mighty though it is, could be obscured; how much more then, other beings!"

## 70. *The Winter Sun*

"Why is the sun more fierce in winter than in summer?"[2]

"In the winter the sky is clear so the sun shines fiercely but in the summer dust rises up and clouds accumulate in the sky so the heat of the sun is reduced."

---

[1] *cf.* Vin. ii. 295, A. ii. 53. "Obscured by four things, O monks, the sun does not shine fiercely; by storm clouds, by mist, by dust clouds, or by eclipse. Obscured by four things recluses do not shine; by drinking intoxicants, by sexual relations, by accepting gold and silver, by wrong livelihood." Hence this dilemma is not at all out of place here. *See* quotations.

[2] Usually three seasons are recognised. What is described as the summer is more like the rainy season than the hot season.

# CHAPTER FIFTEEN

## THE SOLVING OF DILEMMAS (Contd.)

### 71. The Gift of Vessantara

"Venerable Nāgasena, do all the Bodhisattas give away their wives and children, or was it only Vessantara?"[1]

"All of them do."

"But do those wives and children consent to it?"

"The wives do but the children do not due to their tender age."

"But was it then a meritorious deed if the children were terrified and cried at being given away?"

"Yes it was. As a man desiring merit might take a cripple wherever he wanted to go in an ox-cart and thereby the oxen would be made to suffer; or as a king might levy a tax in order to perform a great meritorious deed; so too, giving, though it may cause anguish to some, is conducive to rebirth in heaven. Is there, O king, any gift that should not be given?"

"Yes, Nāgasena, there are ten kinds of gifts that should not be given, the giving of which leads to rebirth in states of woe: a gift of intoxicants, of a festival, of women, of men,[2] of suggestive designs, weapons, poisons, chains or instruments of torture, fowls and swine, or false weights and measures."

"I am not asking about gifts that are not approved of in the world. I am asking if there is any gift that should not be given when there is someone worthy of it."

"Then, Nāgasena, there is no gift that should not be given. When satisfaction in Dhamma has arisen, some people give a hundred thousand, or a kingdom or even their life."

"Then why do you criticize the gift of Vessantara so harshly? Is it not sometimes the case that a man in debt may sell his son or leave him

---

[1] *Jā. vi. 479 ff.*

[2] *Usabha,* according to the PED, is a bull which is the leader of the herd or a very strong man. Ven. Ledi Sayādaw (*Bodhipakkhiya Dīpanī,* Manuals of Buddhism p.200) describes *usabha* as a very special bull, which can protect the whole herd and even the village from disease, hence perhaps the reason why it should not be given away. However, in the above context a gift of men would be more consistent with a gift of women, neither of which would be proper.

as a pledge? Just so, Vessantara gave his son as a pledge against his future attainment of omniscience."

"Nevertheless, why did he not give himself instead?"

"Because that was not what was asked for. To offer something else would have been ignoble. Furthermore, O king, Vessantara knew that the Brahmin would be unable to keep the children as slaves for long since he was advanced in years. Anyway, he knew, their grandfather would pay a ransom for their return."

"Skilfully, Nāgasena, has this puzzle been unravelled. The net of heresy has been torn to pieces. Well has the letter of the scriptures been maintained while you have thus explained the spirit. This is so and I accept it as you say."

## 72. *Austerities*

"Do all Bodhisattas practise austerities or was it only the Bodhisatta Gotama?"

"It was only the Bodhisatta Gotama.[1] In four respects there are differences between Bodhisattas. As to family (either warrior or priestly caste), length of time to develop the perfections, life-span, and height. However, there is no difference between the Buddhas in respect of their virtue or wisdom. It was in order to bring his knowledge to maturity that he had to practise the austerities."

"Why then, Nāgasena, did he go forth while his knowledge was still immature? Why didn't he first mature his knowledge and then renounce the world?"

"When the Bodhisatta, O king, saw the women of his harem sleeping in disorder then he became disgusted and discontented. On perceiving that his mind was filled with discontent, Māra said, 'Seven days from now you will become a Universal Monarch'. Yet, as if a red-hot iron bar had entered his ear, the Bodhisatta was filled with alarm and fear. Furthermore, O king, the Bodhisatta thought, 'Let me not incur blame among gods and men as being without occupation or means. Let me be a man of action and constant in earnestness.' Thus did the Bodhisatta undertake the austerities to bring his knowledge to maturity."

---

[1] M. Sta. 81, Ap. 301. As a result of abusing Buddha Kassapa in a former birth. *See* Dilemma 46.

"Venerable Nāgasena, when the Bodhisatta was undergoing austerities it occurred to him 'Might there not be some other path to higher knowledge worthy of noble men?' Was he then confused about the correct way?"

"There are twenty-five conditions, O king, that cause weakness of mind:[1] anger, enmity, hypocrisy, conceit, envy, avarice, deceit, treachery, obstinacy, perverseness, pride, vanity, conceit, heedlessness, sloth, drowsiness, laziness, evil friends, sights, sounds, odours, tastes, sensations of touch, hunger, thirst, and discontent. It was hunger and thirst that seized hold of his body and thus his mind was not rightly directed to the destruction of the floods *(āsava)*. The Bodhisatta had sought after the perception of the Four Noble Truths for many aeons so how could there arise any confusion in his mind as to the way? Nevertheless, he thought, 'Might there not be some other way to wisdom?' Formerly the Bodhisatta, when he was only one month old, had attained the four absorptions while meditating under the rose-apple tree while his father was ploughing."[2]

"Very good, Nāgasena, I accept it as you say. It was while bringing his knowledge to maturity that the Bodhisatta practised the austerities."

## 73. *The Power of Evil*

"Which is more powerful, wholesomeness or unwholesomeness?"[3]

"Wholesomeness is more powerful, O king."

"That is something I cannot believe for those who do evil often experience the result of their deeds in this very life when they are punished for their crimes,[4] but is there anyone who, by offering alms to the Order or by observing the *Uposatha* has received the benefit in this very life?"

"There are, O king, six[5] such cases. The slave Puṇṇaka,[6] on giving a meal to Sāriputta, attained on the same day to the dignity of a

---

[1] *See* quotations.

[2] M. i. 246, Jā. i. 57.

[3] *cf.* Question 7 in Chapter Seven.

[4] The king is jumping to conclusions to say that criminals are experiencing the results of their evil deeds when they are punished. *See* Dilemma 8; "Without a Buddha's insight no one can ascertain the extent of the action of *kamma*."

[5] Seven, including five of these six, are referred to in Dilemma 4; the extra ones are Puṇṇa the worker and Puṇṇā the slave-girl. The one here not referred to above is Puṇṇaka the slave.

[6] *Dāso* and *dāsi* refer to slaves; *bhātako* was one who worked for a wage.

treasurer. Then there was the mother of Gopāla, who sold her hair and therewith gave a meal to Mahā Kaccāyana and as a result became the chief queen of King Udena. The pious woman Suppiyā, who cut flesh from her own thigh to provide meat for a sick monk but on the very next day the wound healed. Mallikā, when a slave girl, gave her own gruel to the Blessed One and became, that very day, the chief queen of Kosala. Sumana the florist, who presented eight bunches of jasmine to the Blessed One, came into great prosperity and Ekasāṭaka the Brahman who gave the Blessed One his only garment and received that day the gift of 'All the Eights'."[1]

"So then, Nāgasena, for all your searching have you found only six cases?"

"That is so, O king."

"Then it is unwholesomeness that is more powerful than wholesomeness. For I have seen many men impaled on a stake for their crimes, and in the war waged by the general Bhaddasāla in the service of the Nanda royal family against Chandagutta there were eighty Corpse Dances, for they say that when a great slaughter has taken place the headless corpses rise and dance over the battle-field. All of those men came to destruction through the fruit of their evil deeds. Yet when King Pasenadi of Kosala gave the unparalleled alms-giving did he receive wealth or glory or happiness in the same life?"

"No, O king, he did not."

"Then surely, Nāgasena, unwholesomeness is more powerful?"

"Just, O king, as an inferior grain ripens in a month or two but the best grain ripens only after five or six months, good deeds ripen only after a long time. Furthermore, O king, the results of both good and evil will be experienced in a future life, but because evil is blameworthy it has been decreed that those who do evil will be punished by the law, yet they do not reward those who do good. If they were to make a law to reward the good doer then good deeds would also be rewarded in this very life."

"Very good, Nāgasena, only by one as wise as you could this puzzle be so well solved. The question put by me from the ordinary viewpoint has been made clear by you in the supramundane sense."

---

[1] Eight elephants, eight horses, eight thousand *kahāpaṇas*, eight women, eight slaves, and the proceeds from eight villages.

## 74. *Sharing of Merit*

"Is it possible for all deceased relatives to share in the merit of a good deed?"

"No. Only those who are born as hungry ghosts who feed off the merit of others are able to share in the merit. Those born in hell, those in heaven, animals, and hungry ghosts who feed on vomit, or hungry ghosts who hunger and thirst, or hungry ghosts who are consumed by craving, do not derive any profit."

"Then the offerings in those cases are fruitless since those for whom they were given derive no profit."

"No, O king, they are not fruitless nor without result for the givers themselves derive benefit from it."

"Convince me of this by a reason."

"If some people prepared a meal and visited their relatives but those relatives did not accept the gift, would that gift be wasted?"

"No, venerable sir, the owners themselves would have it."

"Just so, O king, the givers derive benefit from their alms-giving."

"Is it then possible to share demerit?"

"This is not a question you should ask, O king. You will be asking me next why space is boundless and why men and birds have two legs whilst deer have four!"

"I do not ask you this to annoy you, but there are many people in the world who are perverted[1] or who lack common sense."[2]

"Though it is possible to ripen a crop with water from a tank it is not possible to use seawater. An evil deed cannot be shared with one who has not done it and has not consented to it. People convey water long distances by means of an aqueduct but they cannot convey solid rock in the same way. Unwholesomeness is a mean thing but wholesomeness is great."

"Give me an illustration."

"If a tiny drop of water were to fall on the ground would it flow over ten or twelve leagues?"

"Certainly not, it would only affect the spot where it fell."

"Why is that?"

"Because of its minuteness."

---

[1] *Vāmagāmino; pāpagāhino* Evil-minded, who take hold of things wrongly.

[2] *Vicakkhukā* — literally without eyes, (or perhaps just plain stupid).

"Just so, O king, unwholesomeness is a mean thing and because of its minuteness affects only the doer and cannot be shared. However, if there was a mighty cloudburst would the water spread around?"

"Certainly, venerable sir, even for ten or twelve leagues."

"Just so, O king, wholesomeness is great and by reason of its abundance can be shared by gods and men."

"Venerable Nāgasena, why is it that unwholesomeness is so limited and wholesomeness so much more far-reaching?"

"Whoever, O king, gives gifts, observes the precepts and performs the *Uposatha,* he is glad and at peace, and being peaceful his goodness grows even more abundantly. Like a deep pool of water from which as soon as water flows away on one side it is replenished from all around. Just so, O king, if a man were to transfer to others the merit of any good he had done even for a hundred years the more would his goodness grow. This is why wholesomeness is so great. However, on doing evil, O king, a man becomes filled with remorse and his mind cannot escape from the thought of it, he is depressed and obtains no peace, miserable and despairing he wastes away. Just, O king, as a drop of water falling onto a dry river-bed gains not in volume but is swallowed up on the very spot where it fell. This is why unwholesomeness is so mean and minute."

## 75. *Dreams*

"What is this thing that people call a dream and who dreams it?"

"It is a sign coming across the path of the mind. There are six kinds of dreams. A person affected by wind sees a dream, a person affected by bile, by phlegm, by a deity, by their own habits, by a premonition. It is only the last of these that is true, all the others are false."

"When one dreams a dream is one awake or asleep?"

"Neither one nor the other. One dreams when one sleeps 'the monkey's sleep', which is midway between sleep and consciousness."

## 76. *Premature Death*

"Venerable Nāgasena, do all living beings die when their life-span comes to an end or do some die prematurely?"

"Both, O king. Like fruits on a tree that fall sometimes when ripe and sometimes before they are ripe due to the wind, or insects or sticks, so too, some beings die when their life-span ends but others die prematurely."

"But Nāgasena, all those who die prematurely, whether they are young or old, have reached the end of their predetermined life-span. There is no such thing as premature death."

"O king, there are seven kinds of premature death for those who, though they still have some life-span remaining, die prematurely: starvation, thirst, snake-bite, poison, fire, drowning, weapons. Death come about in eight ways: through wind, bile, phlegm, a mixture of bodily fluids, change of temperature, stress of circumstances, outside agent, and *kamma*.[1] Of these, only that through *kamma* can be called the end of the life-span; the rest are all premature."

"Venerable Nāgasena, you say there is premature death. Give me another reason for that."

"A mighty fire, O king, that is exhausted and goes out when its fuel has been totally consumed and not before that by some other reason, is said to have gone out in the fullness of time. Just so a man who dies in old-age without any accident is said to reach the end of the life-span. However, in the case of a fire that is put out by a mighty cloudburst it could not be said that it had gone out in the fullness of time; so too whoever dies before his time due to any cause other than *kamma* is said to die a premature death."

## 77. *Miracles at Shrines of Arahants*

"Are there miracles at the shrines *(cetiya)* of all the *arahants* or only at some?"

"Only at some. By the volitional determination of three kinds of individuals there is a miracle: by an *arahant* while he is still alive, by deities, or by a wise disciple who has confidence. If there is no such volitional determination then there is no miracle even at the shrine of an *arahant* who had supernormal powers. However, even if there is no miracle one should have confidence after knowing about his pure and blameless conduct."

## 78. *Can Everyone Understand the Dhamma?*

"Do all those who practise correctly attain insight into the Dhamma or are there some who do not?"

"There can be no attaining of insight for those who, though they practise correctly, are animals, hungry ghosts, holders of wrong views,

---

[1] *See* Dilemma 8.

frauds, matricides, patricides, murderers of *arahants,* schismatics, shedders of the blood of a Tathāgata, in the robes by theft,[1] who have gone over to another sect, who are violators of nuns, are concealing an offence entailing a meeting of the Order,[2] who are eunuchs or hermaphrodites. Neither is a child under seven years of age able to realise the Dhamma."

"What is the reason that a child under seven years of age is unable to attain insight? For a child is pure in mind and should be ready to realise the Dhamma."

"If a child under seven, O king, could feel desire for things leading to desire, hatred for things arousing hatred, could be fooled by misleading things and could distinguish between wholesomeness and unwholesomeness then insight might be possible for him. However, the mind of a child under seven, O king, is feeble and the unconditioned element of *nibbāna* is weighty and profound. Therefore, O king, although he practised correctly, a child of under seven could not realise the Dhamma."

## 79. *The Bliss of Nibbāna*

"Is *nibbāna* entirely blissful or is it partly painful?"

"It is entirely blissful."

"But that I cannot accept. Those who seek it have to practise austerity and exertion of body and mind, abstention from food at the wrong time, suppression of sleep, restraint of the senses, and they have to give up wealth, family and friends. They are blissful who enjoy the pleasures of the senses but you restrain and prevent such pleasures and so experience physical and mental discomfort and pain."

"O king, *nibbāna* has no pain; what you call pain is not *nibbāna*. It is true that those who seek *nibbāna* experience pain and discomfort but afterwards they experience the unalloyed bliss of *nibbāna*. I will tell you a reason for that. Is there, O king, such a thing as the bliss of the sovereignty of kings?"

"Yes there is."

"Is it mixed with pain?"

"No."

"But why is it then, O king, that when the frontier provinces have revolted kings have to set out from their palaces and march over

---

[1] Vin. i. 86. Putting on the robe himself he pretends to be a monk.

[2] Oddly, no mention is made in this list of those guilty of *Pārājika* offences but they could be included as frauds.

uneven ground, tormented by mosquitoes and hot winds, and engage in fierce battles at the risk of their lives?"

"That, venerable Nāgasena, is not the bliss of sovereignty. It is only the preliminary stage in the pursuit of that bliss. It is after they have won it that they enjoy the bliss of sovereignty. That bliss, Nāgasena, is not mixed with pain."

"Just so, O king, *nibbāna* is unalloyed bliss and there is no pain mixed in it."

## 80. *Description of Nibbāna*

"Is it possible, Nāgasena, to point out the size, shape or duration of *nibbāna* by a simile?"

"No it is not possible; there is no other thing like it."

"Is there then any attribute of *nibbāna* found in other things that can be demonstrated by a simile?"

"Yes that can be done.

"As a lotus is unwetted by water, *nibbāna* is unsullied by the defilements.

"Like water, it cools the fever of defilements and quenches the thirst of craving.

"Like medicine, it protects beings who are poisoned by the defilements, cures the disease of suffering, and nourishes like nectar.

"As the ocean is empty of corpses, *nibbāna* is empty of all defilements; as the ocean is not increased by all the rivers that flow into it, so *nibbāna* is not increased by all the beings who attain it; it is the abode of great beings [the *arahants*], and it is decorated with the waves of knowledge and freedom.

"Like food, which sustains life, *nibbāna* drives away old age and death; it increases the spiritual strength of beings; it gives the beauty of virtue, it removes the distress of the defilements, it relieves the exhaustion of all suffering.

"Like space, it is not born, does not decay or perish, it does not pass away here and arise elsewhere, it is invincible, thieves cannot steal it, it is not attached to anything, it is the sphere of ariyans who are like birds in space, it is unobstructed and it is infinite.

"Like a wish-fulfilling gem, it fulfils all desires, causes delight and is lustrous.

"Like red sandalwood, it is hard to get, its fragrance is incomparable and it is praised by good men.

"As ghee is recognisable by its special attributes, so *nibbāna* has special attributes; as ghee has a sweet fragrance, *nibbāna* has the sweet fragrance of virtue; as ghee has a delicious taste, *nibbāna* has the delicious taste of freedom.

"Like a mountain peak, it is very high, immovable, inaccessible to the defilements, it has no place where defilements can grow, and it is without favouritism or prejudice."

## 81. *The Realisation of Nibbāna*

"You say, Nāgasena, that *nibbāna* is neither past, nor present nor future, neither arisen, nor not arisen, nor producible.[1] In that case does the man who realises *nibbāna* realise something already produced, or does he himself produce it first and then realise it?"

"Neither of these, O king, yet *nibbāna* does exist."

"Do not, Nāgasena, answer this question by making it obscure! Make it clear and elucidate it. It is a point on which people are bewildered and lost in doubt. Break this dart of uncertainty."

"The element of *nibbāna* does exist, O king, and he who practises rightly and who rightly comprehends the formations according to the teachings of the Conqueror, he, by his wisdom, realises *nibbāna*.

"How is *nibbāna* to be shown? By freedom from distress and danger, by purity and by coolness. As a man, afraid and terrified at having fallen among enemies, would be relieved and blissful when he had escaped to a safe place; or as one fallen into a pit of filth would be at ease and glad when he had got out of the pit and cleaned up; or as one trapped in a forest fire would be calm and cool when he had reached a safe spot. As fearful and terrifying should you regard the anxiety that arises again and again on account of birth, old age, disease and death; as filth should you regard gain, honours and fame; as hot and searing should you regard the three-fold fire of desire, hatred and delusion.

"How does he who is practising rightly realise *nibbāna?* He rightly grasps the cyclic nature of formations and therein he sees only birth, old age, disease and death; he sees nothing pleasant or agree-

---

[1] Untraced. However, *cf.* Dilemma 65. *See also* quotations.

able in any part of it. Seeing nothing there to be taken hold of, as on a red-hot iron ball, his mind overflows with discontent and a fever takes hold of his body; hopeless and without a refuge he becomes disgusted with repeated lives. To him who sees the terror of the treadmill of life the thought arises, 'On fire and blazing is this wheel of life, full of suffering and despair. If only there could be an end to it, that would be peaceful, that would be excellent; the cessation of all mental formations, the renunciation of grasping, the destruction of craving, dispassion, cessation, *nibbāna!*'

"Therewith his mind leaps forward into the state where there is no becoming. Then has he found peace, then does he exult and rejoice at the thought, 'A refuge has been found at last!' He strives along the path for the cessation of formations, searches it out, develops it, and makes much of it. To that end he stirs up his mindfulness, energy and joy; and from attending again and again to that thought [of disgust with mental formations], having transcended the treadmill of life, he brings the cycle to a halt. One who stops the treadmill is said to have realised *nibbāna.*"

## 82. *Where is Nibbāna?*

"Is there a place, Nāgasena, where *nibbāna* is stored up?"

"No there is not, yet it does exist. As there is no place where fire is stored up yet it may be produced by rubbing two dry sticks together."

"But is there any place on which a man might stand and realise *nibbāna?*"

"Yes there is; virtue is the place;[1] standing on that, and with reasoning, wherever he might be, whether in the land of the Scythians or the Bactrians, whether in China or Tibet,[2] in Kashmir or Gandhāra, on a mountain top or in the highest heavens; the one who practises rightly realises *nibbāna.*"

"Very good, Nāgasena, you have taught about *nibbāna,* you have explained about the realisation of *nibbāna,* you have praised the qualities of virtue, shown the right way of practice, raised aloft the banner of the Dhamma, established the Dhamma as a leading principle, not barren nor without fruit are the efforts of those with right aims!"

---

[1] *cf.* above Question 9 in Chapter One.

[2] *Cilāta* is possibly Tibet. See *Geography of Early Buddhism*, B.C. Law.

# CHAPTER SIXTEEN

## 1. A Question Solved by Inference

Milinda the king went up to the place where Nāgasena was and, having paid respect to him, sat down at one side. Longing to know, to hear and to bear in mind, and wishing to dispel his ignorance, he roused up his courage and energy, established self-possession and mindfulness and spoke thus to Nāgasena:

"Have you, venerable Nāgasena, ever seen the Buddha?"[1]

"No, great king."

"Then have your teachers ever seen the Buddha?"

"No, great king."

"So, Nāgasena, the Buddha did not exist; there is no clear evidence of the Buddha's existence."

"Did those warriors exist who were the founders of the line of kings from which you are descended?"

"Certainly, venerable sir, there can be no doubt about that."

"Have you ever seen them?"

"No, venerable sir."

"Have your teachers and ministers of state who lay down the law ever seen them?"

"No, venerable sir."

"Then there is no clear evidence of the existence of those warriors of old."

"Nevertheless, Nāgasena, the royal insignia used by them are still to be seen and by these we can infer and know that the warriors of old really existed."

"Just so, O king, we can know that the Blessed One lived and believe in him. The royal insignia used by him are still to be seen. There are the four foundations of mindfulness, the four right efforts, the four bases of success, the five moral powers, the five controlling faculties, the seven factors of enlightenment and the eight factors of the path; and by these we can infer and know that the Blessed One really existed."

"Give me an illustration."

---

[1] *cf.* D. i. Sta. 13.

"As people seeing a fine, well-planned city would know it was laid out by a skilled architect; so the city of righteousness laid out by the Blessed One can be seen. It has constant mindfulness for its main street, and in that main street market-stalls are open selling flowers, perfume, fruits, antidotes, medicines, nectar, precious jewels and all kinds of merchandise. Thus, O king, the Blessed One's city of righteousness is well-planned, strongly built, well protected and thus impregnable to enemies; and by this method of inference you may know that the Blessed One existed."

*"What are the flowers in the city of righteousness?"*

"There are meditation objects made known by the Blessed One: the perception of impermanence, of unsatisfactoriness, soullessness, repulsiveness, danger, abandoning, dispassion, disenchantment with all worlds, the impermanence of all mental formations; the meditation on mindfulness of breathing, the perception of the nine kinds of corpses in progressive stages of decay, the meditations on loving-kindness, compassion, sympathetic-joy and equanimity; mindfulness of death and mindfulness of the thirty-two parts of the body.[1] Whoever, longing to be free from old age and death, takes one of these as the subject for meditation can become free from desire, hatred and delusion, pride and wrong views, he can cross the ocean of *saṃsāra,* stem the torrent of craving and destroy all suffering. He can then enter the city of *nibbāna* where there is security, calm and bliss."

*"What are the perfumes in the city of righteousness?"*

They are the undertaking of the restraints of the three refuges, the five precepts, the eight precepts, the ten precepts, and the *Pātimokkha* restraint for monks. For this was said by the Blessed One:

> "No flower's scent can waft against the wind,
> Nor sandalwood's, nor musk's, nor jasmine flower's.
> But the fragrance of the good goes against the wind
> In all directions the good man's name pervades."[2]

---

[1] *See* the glossary.

[2] Dhp. v 54, *see* quotations.

*"What are the fruits in the city of righteousness?"*

"They are the fruit of stream-winner, the fruit of once-returner, the fruit of non-returner, the fruit of *arahantship,* the attainment of emptiness, the attainment of signlessness and the attainment of desirelessness."[1]

*"What is the antidote in the city of righteousness?"*

"The Four Noble Truths are the antidote to counteract the poison of the defilements. Whoever longs for the highest insight and hears this teaching is set free from birth, old age, death, sorrow, pain, grief, lamentation and despair."

*"What is the medicine in the city of righteousness?"*

"Certain medicines, O king, have been made known by the Blessed One by which he cures gods and men. They are these: the four foundations of mindfulness, the four right efforts, the four bases of success, the five controlling faculties, the five moral powers, the seven factors of enlightenment, and the eightfold noble path. With these medicines the Blessed One cures men of wrong views, wrong thought, wrong speech, wrong actions, wrong livelihood, wrong effort, wrong mindfulness and wrong concentration. He rids them of desire, hatred and delusion, pride, personality-belief, doubt, restlessness, sloth and torpor, shamelessness and recklessness and all other defilements.

*"What is the nectar in the city of righteousness?"*

"Mindfulness of the body is like nectar, for all beings who are infused with this nectar of mindfulness of the body are relieved of all suffering. For this was said by the Blessed One:

> "They enjoy the nectar of the deathless
> who practise mindfulness of the body."[2]

*"What are the precious jewels in the city of righteousness?"*

"Virtue, concentration, wisdom, freedom, knowledge and vision

---

[1] One with great resolution contemplates impermanence and attains signlessness, one with great tranquillity contemplates unsatisfactoriness and attains desirelessness, one with great wisdom contemplates not-self and attains emptiness.

[2] A. i. 45. *See* quotations.

of freedom, knowledge of discrimination and the factors of enlightenment are the precious jewels of the Blessed One.

"What is the precious jewel of virtue? It is the virtue of restraint by the *Pātimokkha* rules, the virtue of restraint of the sense faculties, the virtue of right livelihood, the virtue of reflection on the proper use of the four requisites of almsfood, medicine, robes and lodgings, the virtue of restraint according to the major, middle and minor codes of discipline[1] and the habitual virtue of the noble ones.

"What is the precious jewel of concentration? It is the first *jhāna* with initial application and sustained application, the second *jhāna* without initial application but with sustained application, the third *jhāna* with neither initial nor sustained application but with pure joy, bliss and one-pointedness; and it is the concentration on emptiness, on signlessness and desirelessness. When a monk wears this jewel of concentration, evil, unprofitable thoughts are shed from his mind like water from a lotus leaf.

"What is the precious jewel of wisdom? It is the knowledge of what is wholesome and what unwholesome, what blameless and what blameworthy, and knowledge of the Four Noble Truths.

"What is the precious jewel of freedom? *Arahantship* is the gem of gems, the precious jewel of freedom adorned with which a monk outshines all others.

"What is the precious jewel of knowledge and vision of freedom? It is the knowledge by which the noble disciple reviews the paths, the fruits and *nibbāna,* and reflects on the defilements that have been got rid of and the defilements that still remain.

"What is the precious jewel of knowledge of discrimination? It is the analytical insight of meaning, law, language and intelligence. Whoever is adorned with this jewel is unafraid when approaching any kind of assembly, confident in the knowledge that he can answer any kind of question that might be put to him.

"What is the precious jewel of the factors of enlightenment? They are the jewels of mindfulness, investigation of truth, energy, joy, tranquillity, concentration and equanimity. Adorned with these jewels the monk illumines the world with his virtuousness."

---

[1] Described in detail in the *Sāmañña Phala Sutta* of the *Dīgha Nikāya,* these disciplines list all kinds of wrong livelihood for a monk such as fortune telling and getting involved in householder's business, and all misbehaviour such as playing games.

## 2. The Ascetic Practices

The king saw monks in the forest, lone and far away from men, keeping hard vows. Then he saw householders at home, enjoying the sweet fruits of the Noble Path. Considering both of these, deep doubts he felt, "If laymen also realise the truth, then surely making vows must be worthless. Come! Let me ask that best of teachers, wise in the threefold collection of the Buddha's words, skilled to overthrow the arguments of the opponents. He will be able to resolve my doubts!"

Milinda approached Nāgasena, paid respects to him, and seated at one side asked: "Venerable Nāgasena, is there any layperson who has attained *nibbāna?*"

"Not only one hundred or a thousand but more than a billion[1] have attained *nibbāna.*"

"If, Nāgasena, laypeople living at home, enjoying the pleasures of the senses can attain *nibbāna* what is the use of the extra vows? If one's enemies could be subdued with fists alone what would be the use of seeking weapons? If trees could be climbed by clambering up what would be the use of ladders? If it was comfortable to lie on the bare ground what would be the use of beds? Just so, if a layperson can attain *nibbāna* even while living at home what is the use of the extra vows?"

"There are, O king, twenty-eight virtues of these practices[2] on account of which the Buddhas have a high regard for them. The keeping of the vows is a pure mode of livelihood, its fruit is blissful, it is blameless, it brings no suffering to others, it gives confidence,[3] it doesn't oppress,[4] it is certain to bring growth in good qualities, it prevents back-sliding, it doesn't delude, it is a protection, it fulfils one's desires, it tames all beings, it is good for self-discipline, it is proper for a recluse, he is independent,[5] he is free,[6] it destroys desire, it destroys hatred, it destroys delusion, it humbles pride, it cuts off

---

[1] As well as human beings there were millions of deities and Brahmās who realised *nibbāna* while listening to the Dhamma.

[2] *See* quotations

[3] He is free from fear of robbers.

[4] That is by the need to protect property.

[5] He is unattached to families.

[6] He is free to go anywhere. Vism. 59-83.

discursive thoughts and makes the mind one-pointed, it overcomes doubts, it drives away sloth, it banishes discontent, it makes him tolerant, it is incomparable, it is beyond measure, and it leads to the destruction of all suffering.

"Whosoever carries out these vows becomes endowed with eighteen good qualities. His conduct is pure, his practice is fully accomplished, his actions and speech are well-guarded, his thoughts are pure, his energy is stirred up, his fear is allayed, views of personality are dispelled, wrath dies away and love arises, he eats perceiving the repulsive nature of food, he is honoured by all beings, he is moderate in eating, he is full of vigilance, he is homeless and can dwell wherever it suits him, he detests evil, he delights in solitude, and he is always heedful.

"These ten individuals are worthy of undertaking the vows: one full of confidence, full of shame, full of courage, void of hypocrisy, one who is self-reliant, steadfast, desirous of training, of strong determination, very introspective, and one who is of a loving disposition.

"All those laypeople who realise *nibbāna* while living at home do so because they practised these vows in former births. There is no realisation of the goal of *arahantship* in this very life without these vows. Only by the utmost zealousness is *arahantship* attained. Thus the value of keeping the vows if full of value and might.

"Whosoever, O king, having evil desires in his mind, should take upon himself these vows seeking after material gain shall incur a double punishment; in this world he will be scorned and ridiculed and after death he will suffer in hell.

"Whosoever, O king, whose conduct is consistent with monkhood, who is worthy of it, who desires little and is content, given to seclusion, energetic, without guile, and has gone forth not from desire for gain or fame but with confidence in the Dhamma, wishing for deliverance from old age and death, he is worthy of double honour for he is loved by gods and men and he quickly attains the four fruits, the four kinds of discrimination,[1] the three-fold vision[2] and the sixfold higher knowledge.[3]

---

[1] Discrimination of meaning, law, language and intelligence.

[2] *Tevijjā* — Recollection of past lives, knowledge of the arising and passing away of beings, knowledge of destruction of the floods *(āsava)*.

[3] *Abhiññāṇa* — Supernormal power such as flying through the air, the divine ear or clairaudience, penetration of minds, plus the above three.

"What are the thirteen vows? Wearing rag-robes, using only three robes, living only on alms-food, begging from house to house without preference, eating one meal a day, eating from the bowl only, refusing later food, dwelling in the forest, dwelling at the root of a tree, dwelling in the open, dwelling in a cemetery, using any sleeping place allotted to him, and not lying down to sleep.[1]

"It was by the observance of these vows that Upasena was able to visit the Blessed One when he was dwelling in solitude[2] and it was by these same vows that Sāriputta became of such exalted virtue that he was declared second only to the Blessed One himself in ability to preach the Dhamma."[3]

"Very good, Nāgasena, the whole teaching of the Buddha, the supramundane attainments and all the best achievements in the world are included in these thirteen ascetic practices."

---

[1] *See* Vism. 59ff, for details.

[2] Vin. iii. 230ff.

[3] A. i. 23, *cf.* S. i. 191.

# CHAPTER SEVENTEEN

## The Similes

"Venerable Nāgasena, with which qualities must a monk be endowed in order to realise *arahantship?*"[1]

### 1. *The Donkey*

"Just, O king, as the donkey, wherever he may lie down, does not rest long; so should the monk who is intent on *arahantship* not rest long."

### 2. *The Cockerel*

"As the cockerel goes to roost at the proper time; so should the monk quickly perform his duties[2] after the almsround and enter a solitary place for meditation.

"As the cockerel rises early; so should the monk rise early.

"As the cockerel constantly scratches the ground in search of food; so should the monk constantly reflect on the food he takes reminding himself, 'I eat this not for enjoyment, nor for complexion, but merely to appease the pain of hunger and to enable me to practise the holy life, thus I shall put an end to sorrow'.

"As the cockerel, though it has eyes, is blind at night; so should the monk while meditating be as if blind, paying no attention to sense objects that might disturb his concentration.

"As the cockerel, even though driven off with sticks and stones, will not desert his roost; so should the monk not give up his mindfulness whether he is engaged in making robes, in building, teaching, studying the scriptures, or in other work.

---

[1] In the Pali text, 67 similes are given but some of them are repetitive and others rely for their effectiveness on a play on words in Pali which is difficult to translate so I have only included a selection here. The numbering, however, has been retained to make cross-reference easier.

[2] As a point of interest one of the duties mentioned is sweeping the surround to the *cetiya* or pagoda. In the time of Asoka some 84,000 were built in India but above in Dilemma 25 honouring the remains of the Tathāgata was not the duty of monks. In the *Mahāyāna Vinaya* there are a number of extra minor training rules relating to the proper conduct with regard to *cetiyas*.

## 4. *The Female Panther*

"As the panther conceives only once and does not resort again to the male; so should the monk, seeing the suffering inherent in rebirth, resolve not to enter on any future existence. For this was said by the Buddha, O king, in the *Dhaniya Sutta* of the *Sutta Nipāta:*

> "Having broken the fetters like a bull, as an elephant having broken the creepers, so there will be no more rebirth for me. Therefore, rain, O cloud, if you like!"[1]

## 7. *The Bamboo*

"As the bamboo bends whichever way the wind blows; so should the monk be flexible and conform to the teaching.

## 10. *The Monkey*

"As the monkey dwells in a mighty tree, well covered with branches; so should the monk dwell with a learned teacher, who is worthy of veneration and able to instruct him.

## 12. *The Lotus*

"As the lotus remains undefiled by the water in which it is born and grows; so should the monk be undefiled by support, offerings and veneration.

"As the lotus remains lifted far above the water; so should the monk remain far above worldly things.

"As the lotus trembles in the slightest breeze; so should the monk tremble at the mere thought of doing any evil, seeing danger in the slightest fault.

## 20. *The Ocean*

"As the ocean casts out corpses on the shore; so should the monk cast out defilements from his mind.

"As the ocean, though it contains many treasures, does not cast them up; so should the monk possess the gems of the attainments but not display them.

---

[1] Sn. v 29. Trnsl. Hammalawa Saddhātissa.

"As the ocean associates with mighty creatures; so should the monk associate with those fellow disciples who are of few desires, virtuous, learned and wise.

"As the ocean does not overflow its shore; so should the monk never transgress the precepts even for the sake of his life.

"As the ocean is not filled up even by all the rivers that flow into it; so should the monk never be satiated with hearing the teaching and instruction in the *Dhamma, Vinaya* and *Abhidhamma*.

## 21. *The Earth*

"As the great earth is unmoved by fair or foul things thrown down on it; so should the monk remain unmoved by praise or blame, support or neglect.

"As the great earth is unadorned but has its own odour; so should the monk be unadorned with perfumes but endowed with the fragrance of his virtue.

"As the great earth is never weary though it bears many things; so should the monk never be weary of giving instruction, exhortation and encouragement.

"As the great earth is without malice or fondness; so should the monk be without malice or fondness.

## 22. *Water*

"As water naturally remains still; so should the monk be without hypocrisy, complaining, hinting, and improper behaviour and remain undisturbed and pure by nature.

"As water always refreshes; so should the monk, full of compassion, always seek the good and benefit of all.

"As water never harms anyone; so should the monk, earnest in effort, never do any wrong that would produce quarrels or strife, or anger or discontent. For it was said by the Blessed One in the *Kaṇha Jātaka*:

> "O Sakka, Lord of all the world, a choice thou bidst
> declare: No creature be aught harmed for me,
> O Sakka, anywhere, Neither in body nor in mind:
> this, Sakka, is my prayer."[1]

---

[1] Jā. iv. 14. PTS trnsl.

## 27. *The Moon*

"As the moon increases day by day in the waxing phase; so should the monk increase in good qualities day by day.

## 30. *The Universal Monarch*

"As the universal monarch gains the favour of the people by the four bases of popularity [generosity, affability, justice and impartiality] so should the monk gain the favour of monks and laity.

"As the universal monarch allows no robbers to dwell in his realm; so should the monk allow no cruel, lustful or angry thought to dwell in his mind.

"As the universal monarch travels all over the world examining the good and the bad; so should the monk examine himself thoroughly as to his thoughts, words and deeds.

## 35. *The Mongoose*

"As the mongoose protects himself with an antidote before approaching a snake; so should the monk protect himself with loving-kindness before approaching the world, which abounds in anger and malice, strife and contention.

## 40. *The Elephant*

"As the elephant turns his whole body when he looks round; so should the monk turn his whole body when he looks round, not glancing this way and that but keeping his eyes well controlled.

"As the elephant lifts up his feet and walks with care; so should the monk be mindful and clearly comprehending in walking.

## 46. *The Indian Crane*

"As the Indian crane warns people about their future fate with his cry; so should the monk warn people about their future fate with his teaching of Dhamma.

## 47. *The Bat*

"As the bat, though he sometimes enters men's houses, soon leaves; so should the monk, though he enters men's houses for alms, soon leave.

"As the bat when he frequents men's houses does no harm; so should the monk when visiting men's houses do no harm there being easily supportable and considerate of their welfare.

## *48. The Leech*

"As the leech feeds until he is satisfied before he lets go; so should the monk take a firm hold of his meditation object and drink the delicious nectar of freedom until he is satisfied.

## *50. The Rock Snake*

"As the rock snake can survive for many days without food but still keep himself alive; so should the monk be able to keep himself going even though he receives only a little alms. For this was said by Venerable Sāriputta:

> "Whether it be dry food or wet he eats, let him to full repletion never eat. The good recluse goes forth in emptiness, and keeps to moderation in his food. If but four mouthfuls or five he gets, let him drink water for what cares a man with mind on *arahantship* fixed for ease."[1]

## *60. The Carpenter*

"As the carpenter discards rotten wood and takes only sound timber; so should the monk discard wrong views like eternalism, nihilism, the soul is the body, the soul is one thing the body another, all teachings are alike excellent, the unconditioned is an impossibility, men's actions are useless, there is no holy life, when a being dies a new being is reborn, conditioned things are eternally existing, the one who acts experiences the result thereof, one acts and another experiences the result, and all other such wrong views on the result of *kamma* (intention) and action *(kiriya)*. Having discarded all such paths he should seize the idea of voidness, which is the true nature of conditioned things.[2]

---

[1] Thag. vv 982, 983.

[2] *See* quotations.

## *61. The Waterpot*

"As the waterpot that is full makes no noise; so should the monk be not garrulous even though he knows much, for this was said by the Blessed One:

"Listen to the sound of water.
Listen to the water running through chasms and rocks.
It is the minor streams that make a loud noise,
The great waters flow silently."

"The hollow resounds and the full is still.
Foolishness is like a half-filled pot;
The wise man is a lake full of water.'[1]

On the conclusion of this debate between the elder and the king the great earth shook six times, lightning flashed and the gods rained down flowers from heaven. Milinda was filled with joy of heart and all his pride was subdued. He ceased to have any doubt about the Triple Gem and, renouncing all obstinacy, like a cobra deprived of its fangs he said, "Most excellent, venerable Nāgasena! You have solved the puzzles that were worthy of a Buddha to solve. Among the Budddha's followers there is no one like you, except for Venerable Sāriputta. Please forgive me for my faults. May you accept me as a follower, as one gone for refuge for as long as life lasts."

The king, with his soldiers, supported the elder and his large following and had a dwelling place constructed called Milinda Vihāra. Later, Milinda handed over his kingdom to his son and, going forth into homelessness, he developed his insight and attained *arahantship*.

---

[1] Sn. vv 720, 721, trnsl. Hammalawa Saddhātissa. Only the second verse is quoted in Miln. *See* quotations.

## Dedication

That I have been able to complete this work at all is due to the dedication of Pali scholars like Professor T.W. Rhys Davids and Miss I.B. Horner who have done a great service to all Buddhists, and indeed to all who have any true religious aspirations, by translating the Pali texts into English. As the great engineers and architects of Victorian times have built great railways, canals and bridges and all that remains for us to do is to travel to our destinations, or perhaps now and then to carry out some modernisation work; so this work of mine is only one of modernisation, wishing that present-day readers can more easily acquire a knowledge of Buddhism and come to appreciate the spiritual legacy left for us by the Buddha and his disciples.

Whatever merit I have acquired by my efforts I share with all those scholars who have dedicated their lives to spreading the knowledge of the Buddha's teachings.

With the aid of this merit may I have the power to change those things that should be changed, the patience to tolerate those things that cannot be changed and above all the wisdom to know the difference.

Bhikkhu Pesala 1990

**4 Fruits of the Path**

1. **The Stream-winner** *(sotāpanna)*. On realising *nibbāna* for the first time the stream-winner destroys the three fetters of personality-belief, belief in rites and rituals, and doubts. He is incapable of committing any of the heinous crimes and if he does any other evil he is incapable of concealing it. He is assured of attaining *arahantship* within seven lives at the most.

2. **The Once-returner** *(sakadāgāmi)* greatly reduces the strength of the fetters of desire and ill-will and will, at most, be reborn only once more on earth before attaining *arahantship*.

3. **The Non-returner** *(anāgāmi)* eradicates totally the fetters of desire and ill-will and will not be reborn again on earth but will gain *arahantship* in the higher planes of *devas* or *Brahmās*.

4. **The Arahant** removes the remaining five fetters, destroys all ignorance and craving and puts an end to all forms of rebirth, thus gaining the final goal of the holy life.

**4 Modes of Fearlessness** *(vesārajja)*

The Blessed One said, "I do not see any grounds on which anyone might reprove me as to: 1) being fully awakened, 2) the floods being fully destroyed, 3) knowledge of what is an obstacle to progress, 4) knowledge of Dhamma that leads to the destruction of the floods.

**5 Aggregates of Being** *(khandha)*

When we say 'living being' it is just a conventional way of speaking. Underlying this convention are the wrong views of personality-belief, permanence and substantiality. However, if we consider more carefully what a living being or a person really is we will find only a stream of ever changing phenomena. These can be arranged in five groups: the body or material phenomena; feelings, perceptions, mental formations and consciousness. It should not be understood that these groups are something stable; they are only categories.

**5 Hindrances** *(nīvaraṇa)*

Sensual desire, ill-will, sloth and torpor, restlessness and remorse, doubt. These defilements are called hindrances because they obstruct the development of concentration.

**8 Causes of Earthquakes**

1. This earth is supported by water, the water by air, the air by space. At times great winds blow strongly and the water is shaken. When the water is shaken, the earth is shaken. (N.B. Water is the element of cohesion or fluidity, air the element of motion. These elements are present even in molten rock).
2. A recluse or deity of great power causes the earth to shake by the power of concentration.
3. When the Bodhisatta passes away from the Tusita heaven, mindfully and deliberately, and is conceived in his mother's womb the great earth shakes.
4. When the Bodhisatta issues forth from his mother's womb, mindfully and deliberately, the great earth shakes.
5. When the Tathāgata attains the supreme and perfect enlightenment the great earth shakes.
6. When the Tathāgata sets in motion the wheel of the Dhamma the great earth shakes.
7. When the Tathāgata, mindfully and deliberately, gives up the life-sustaining mental process the great earth shakes. (He could prolong his life by supernormal power but not being asked, he gives up the possibility and announces the time of his death.)
8. When a Buddha passes away and attains *parinibbāna* the great earth shakes.

**10 Fetters** *(saṃyojana)*

Sensual desire *(kāmachanda)*, ill-will *(byāpāda)*, pride *(māna)*, personality-belief *(sakkāyadiṭṭhi)*, doubt *(vicikicchā)*, adherence to rites and ceremonies *(sīlabattaṃ)*, desire for existence *(rūparāga)*, jealousy *(issā)*, avarice *(macchariya)*, ignorance *(avijjā)*.

**10 Perfections** *(pāramī)*

Generosity *(dāna)*, virtue *(sīla)*, renunciation *(nekkhamma)*, wisdom *(paññā)*, energy *(viriya)*, patience *(khanti)*, truthfulness *(sacca)*, determination *(adhiṭṭhāna)*, loving-kindness *(mettā)* and equanimity *(upekkhā)*.

**18 Characteristics of a Buddha** *(Buddhadhammā)*

1-3) Seeing all things; past, present and future. 4-6) Propriety of action, speech and thought. 7-12) Establishment of the following so that they cannot be frustrated by others: intentions, doctrines, that which proceeds from concentration, energy, liberation and wisdom. 13) Avoiding: pleasures or anything that could invite ridicule; 14) Avoiding strife and contention. 15) Omniscience. 16) Doing all things fully conscious. 17) Doing all things with some purpose. 18) Not doing anything from unwise partiality.

**32 Parts of the Body** (for contemplation)

Head hairs, body hairs, nails, teeth, skin; flesh, sinews, bones, bone-marrow, kidneys; heart, liver, membranes, spleen, lungs; large intestine, small intestine, mesentery, gorge, faeces; bile, phlegm, pus, blood, sweat; solid fat, liquid fat, saliva, nasal mucus, synovic fluid, urine, brain.

**Abhidhamma** — the higher teaching. It uses the analytical method. Whereas the discourses use the conventional language of man or being the *Abhidhamma* uses terms like 'five aggregates of being,' mind and matter, visible object and sensitive eye-base *etc.*

**Absorptions** *(jhāna)* — Stages of mental concentration gained by inhibiting the five hindrances. The result of these states is rebirth in the Brahmā realm.

**Austerities** *(dukkarakārikā)* — These are practices of self mortification, which were practised by the Bodhisatta. They should be distinguished from ascetic practices *(dhutaṅga)*, which, although difficult, are neither ignoble nor unprofitable.

**Arahant** — See 4 Fruits of the Path.

**Bactrian Greek** — *(Yonaka)*. There are several references to *Yonaka* other than in the *Milinda Pañha*. An inscription in caves at Nasik, near Bombay refers to nine *Yonaka* who were donors, and the *Mahāvaṃsa* has references to monks from Yona, one Yonadhammarakkhita who must have been a Bactrian Greek *bhikkhu*.

**Bhikkhu** — A Buddhist monk who has received the higher ordination. The literal meaning is 'beggar' though a *bhikkhu* is not allowed to beg, but may only stand and wait for alms to be offered.

**Bodhisatta** — A being totally dedicated to the attainment of the perfect enlightenment of a Buddha, for which one has to develop the perfections for many aeons.

**Bodhi Tree** — The tree under which the Bodhisatta became Buddha. The Ānanda Bodhi Tree was a sapling of the original tree that Ānanda brought to Sāvatthi to remind people of the Buddha when he was away. Another sapling was sent to Sri Lanka by Asoka and is still worshipped.

**Brahmā** — A god or divine being who is in a plane of existence detached from sensuality.

**Brahmacārin** — One who leads a life of chastity.

**Brahman** — A Hindu priest or one of that caste.

**Cāra** (good conduct) is the fulfilment of duties. Its counterpart, *sīla*, is refraining from wrong-doing.

**Merit** *(puññā)* — Good actions that are the basis for happiness and prosperity in the round of rebirths.

**Minor and Lesser Precepts** — The *Pāṭimokkha* rules are arranged in seven groups in order of severity. Offences of Defeat *(pārājika)*, Formal Meeting *(saṅghādisesa)*, Indeterminate *(aniyata)*, Forfeiture *(nissaggiyā pācittiya)*, Expiation *(pācittiya)*, Confession *(patidesaniyā)* and Wrong-doing *(dukkaṭa)*. Wrong speech *(dubhāsita)* is not included in the *Pāṭimokkha* itself but is found elsewhere in the *Vinaya* rule. The author's decision on this matter is very reasonable, since the *pācittiya* rules include killing animals, drinking intoxicants, telling lies, hitting or abusing monks. These could not be called 'minor' training rules that the Buddha might have considered optional after his passing away.

**Non-returner**
**Once-returner** } — See 4 Fruits of the Path.

**Parinibbāna** — The death of a Buddha, Pacceka Buddha or *arahant*.

**Pātimokkha** — The 227 training rules that the monks recite in the *Uposatha* day ceremony every full-moon and new-moon.

**Puthujjana** (Ordinary Person) — A distinction should be made between a blind worldling *(andho puthujjana)* and a well-informed person *(kalyāṇa puthujjana)*. Neither is free from personality belief, but the well-informed person who has faith in the Buddha's enlightenment and believes in *kamma* will cultivate the path to enlightenment. The blind worldling, who holds wrong views, will rarely do wholesome deeds like charity, let alone take up the arduous practice of meditation for concentration or insight.

**Rains** *(vassa)* — The three months from August to October during which the monks remain in one place. A monk's seniority is measured in rains or the number of years he has been a monk.

**Reasoning** *(yoniso manasikāra)* — Often translated as 'Systematic attention'. It means paying attention to the characteristics that reduce defilements rather than to those that increase them.

**Samaṇa** — A recluse or ascetic, not necessarily Buddhist.

**Solitary Buddha** — A Pacceka Buddha or one who attains enlightenment without the help of an Omniscient Buddha. Unlike an Omniscient Buddha, the Solitary Buddha has not fully developed the ability to teach others.

**Stream-winner** — See 4 Fruits of the Path.

**Sutta** — The collection of discourses containing the majority of the Buddha's teaching to both monastics and laity.

**Tipiṭaka** — The threefold collection of *Sutta, Vinaya* and *Abhidhamma; i.e.* discourses, disciplinary rules and philosophy.

**Vedagū** — is used in the *Milinda Pañha* in the sense of a soul or experiencer who sees, hears, smells, tastes, feels or knows. It is also an epithet of the Buddha meaning 'The one who has attained to knowledge'.

**Vinaya** — The six books of the *Tipiṭaka* that deal with the monks' discipline and other regulatory matters.

**Visuddhimagga** — A much respected manual, written in Pali in the 3rd century A.D. by Venerable Buddhaghosa, that elucidates the three-fold training of virtue, concentration and wisdom.

Ch.1 §1 *Yathā hi aṅgasambhāra, hoti saddo ratho iti. Evaṃ khandhesu santesu, hoti 'satto' ti sammutī'ti. (S. i. 135)*

Ch.1 §9 *Sīle patiṭṭhāya naro sapañño, cittaṃ paññañca bhāvayaṃ. Ātāpi nipako bhikkhu, so imaṃ vijaṭaye jaṭa'nti. (S. i. 13)*

Ch.1 §10 *Saddhāya tarati oghaṃ, appamādena aṇṇavaṃ. Vīriyena dukkhamacceti, paññāya parisujjhatī'ti. (S. i. 214)*

Ch.1 §11 *Vīriyavā kho bhikkhave ariyasāvako akusalaṃ pajahati, kusalaṃ bhāveti. Sāvajjaṃ pajahati, anavajjaṃ bhāveti. Suddhamattānaṃ pariharatī'ti. (A. iv. 110)*

Ch.1 §12 *Satiñca khvāhaṃ bhikkhave sabbatthikaṃ vadāmī'ti. (not traced.)*

Ch.1 §13 *Samādhiṃ bhikkhave bhāvetha, samāhito bhikkhave bhikkhu yathābhūtaṃ pajānātī'ti. (S. iii. 13; v. 414)*

Ch.2 §4 *Nābhinandāmi maraṇaṃ, nābhinandāmi jīvitaṃ. Kālañca paṭikaṅkhāmi, nibbisaṃ bhatako yathā. Nābhi ... pe ... paṭikaṅkhāmi, sampajāno patissato'ti. (Thag. 1002,3)*

Ch.3 §3 *Anekajātisaṃsāraṃ sandhāvissaṃ anibbisaṃ gahakāraṃ gavesanto dukkhā jāti punappunaṃ. Gahakārakadiṭṭhosi puna gehaṃ na kāhasi sabbā te phāsukā bhaggā gahakūtaṃ visaṅkhataṃ visaṅkhāragataṃ cittaṃ taṇhānaṃ khayamajjhagā. (Dhp. vv 153,4)*

Ch.4 §2 *Kamassakā māṇava sattā kammadāyāda kammayonī kammabandhū kammappaṭisaraṇā, kammaṃ satte vibhajati yadidaṃ hīnappaṇītatāyā'ti. (M. iii. 203)*

## Dilemma

4. *Aṭṭhime Ānanda hetū aṭṭha paccayā mahato bhūmicālassa pātubhāvāyā'ti. (D. ii. 107; A. iv. 312)*

7. *Pañceva dāni Ānanda vassasatāni [sahassāni] saddhammo ṭhassatī'ti. (Vin. ii. 256; A. iv. 278)*

7. *Ime ca Subhadda bhikkhū sammā vihareyyuṃ, asuñño loko arahantehi assā'ti. (D. ii. 152)*

9. Twenty-eight Advantages of Solitude

*Katame aṭṭhavīsati, idha mahārāja paṭisallānaṃ paṭisallīyamānaṃ attānaṃ rakkhati, āyuṃ vaḍḍeti, balaṃ deti, vajjaṃ padahati, ayasamapaneti, yasamupaneti, aratiṃ vinodeti, ratimupadahati, bhayamapaneti, vesārajjāṃ karoti, kosajjamapaneti, vīriyamabhijaneti, rāgamapaneti, dosamapaneti, mohamapaneti, mānaṃ nihanti, vitakkaṃ bhañjati, cittaṃ ekaggaṃ karoti, mānasaṃ snehayati (samanupassantā),*[1] *hāsaṃ janeti, garukaṃ karoti, lābhamuppādayati, namassiyaṃ karoti, pītiṃ pāpeti, pāmojjaṃ karoti, saṅkhārānaṃ sabhāvaṃ dassayati, bhavappaṭisandhiṃ ugghāṭeti, sabbasāmaññaṃ deti.*

10. *Tathāgatassa kho Ānanda cattāro iddhipādā bhāvitā bahulīkatā yānīkatā vatthukatā anuṭṭhitā paricitā susamāraddhā, so ākaṅkhamāno Ānanda Tathāgato kappaṃ vā tiṭṭheyya kappāvasesaṃ vā'ti. (D. ii. 103; S. v. 259)*

10. *Ito tiṇṇaṃ māsānaṃ accayena tathāgato parinibbāyissatī'ti. (D. ii. 119; S. v. 262)*

10. *Seyyathāpi bhikkhave appamattakopi gūtho duggandho hoti. Evameva kho ahaṃ bhikkhave appamattakampi bhavaṃ na vaṇṇemi antamaso accharāsaṅghātamattampī'ti. (A. i. 34)*

11. *Abhiññāyāhaṃ bhikkhave dhammaṃ desemi no anabhiññāyā'ti. (A. i. 276)*

11. *Ākaṅkhamāno Ānanda saṅgho mamaccayena khuddānukhuddakāni sikkhāpadāni samūhanatū'ti. (D. ii. 154)*

---

[1] *Sinhalese text.*

12. *Natthānanda tathāgatassa dhammesu ācariyamuṭṭhī'ti.* (D. ii. 100)

13. *Sabbe tasanti daṇḍassa, sabbe bhāyanti maccuno'ti.* (Dhp. v 129)

13. *Arahā sabbabhayamatikkanto'ti.* (Untraced but cf. S. i. 125; Thag 707.)

14. *Na antalikkhe na samuddamajjhe, na pabbatānaṃ vivaraṃ pavissa. Na vijjatī so jagatippadeso, yatthaṭṭhito mucceyya maccupāsā'ti.* (Dhp. v 128)

15. *Lābhī tathāgato cīvara-piṇḍapāta-senāsana-gilānappaccaya-bhesajja-parikkhārāna'nti.* (Untraced)

15. *Pañcasālaṃ brahmaṇagāmaṃ piṇḍāya pavisitvā kiñcideva alabhitvā yathādhotena pattena nikkhanto'ti.* (S. i. 113f)

16. *Yo ajānanto pāṇātipātaṃ karoti, so balavataraṃ apuññaṃ pasavatī'ti.* (Untraced)

16.— *anāpatti ajānantassā'ti.* (Vin. iii.78)

17. *Tathāgatassa kho Ānanda na evaṃ hoti, "Ahaṃ bhikkhusaṅghaṃ pariharissāmī"ti.* (D. ii. 100)

17. *So anekasahassaṃ bhikkhusaṅghaṃ pariharissati, seyyathāpi ahaṃ etarahi anekasataṃ bhikkhusaṅghaṃ pariharāmi'ti.* (D. iii. 76)

18. *Tathāgato abhejjapariso'ti.* (D. iii. 172)

18. *Devadattena ekappahāraṃ pañca bhikkhusatāni bhinnānī'ti.* (Vin. ii. 199)

19. *Dhammo hi Vāseṭṭha seṭṭho janetasmiṃ diṭṭhe ceva dhamme abhisamparāye cā'ti.* (D. iii. 93ff.)

19. *Upāsakogihīsotāpanno pihitāpāyodiṭṭhippatto viññātasāsano bhikkhuṃ vā sāmaṇeraṃ vā puthujjanaṃ abhivādeti paccuṭṭhetī'ti.* (Miln. 162)

19. Twenty Qualities of a Recluse

*Katame vīsati samaṇassa samaṇakaraṇā dhammā dve ca liṅgāni, seṭṭho (seṭṭhabhūmisayo): dhammārāmo, aggo niyamo, cāro, vihāro, saṃyamo, saṃvaro, khanti, soraccaṃ, ekattacariyā, ekattābhirati, paṭisallānaṃ, hiri-ottappaṃ, vīriyaṃ, appamādo, sikkhāsamādānaṃ (sikkhāpadhānaṃ), uddeso, paripucchā, sīlādi-abhirati, nirālayatā, sikkhāpadapāripūritā; kāsāvadhāraṇaṃ, bhaṇḍubhāvo.*

20. *Tathāgato sabbasattānaṃ ahitamapanetvā hitam-upaḍahatī'ti. (cf. A. i. 20)*

20. *Saṭṭhimattānaṃ bhikkhūnaṃ uṇhaṃ lohitaṃ mukhato uggata'nti. (A. iv. 128 ff.)*

21. *Kāyena saṃvaro sādhu, sādhu vācāya saṃvaro. Manasā saṃvaro sādhu, sādhu sabbattha saṃvaro'ti. (S. i. 73; Dhp. v 361)*

21. *Selassa brahmaṇassa kosohitaṃ vattaguyhaṃ dassesi. (M. Sta. 92)*

22. *Parisuddhavacīsamācāro āvuso tathāgato, natthi Tathāgatassa vacīduccaritaṃ, yaṃ tathāgato rakkheyya, "Mā me idaṃ paro aññāsī"ti. (D. iii. 217)*

22. *Moghapurisa. (Vin. iii. 20)*

23. *Acetanaṃ brāhmaṇa assuṇantaṃ, jāno ajānantamimaṃ palāsaṃ. Āraddhavīriyo dhuvaṃ appamatto, sukhaseyyaṃ pucchasi kissa hetū'ti. (Jā. iii. 24)*

23. *Iti phandanarukkhopi, tāvade ajjhabhāsatha. Mayhampi vacanaṃ atthi, bhāradvāja suṇohi me'ti. (Jā. iv. 210)*

24. *Cundassa bhattaṃ bhuñjitvā, kammārassāti me sutaṃ. Ābādhaṃ samphusī dhīro, pabāḷhaṃ māraṇantika'nti. (D. ii. 128)*

24. *Dve'me Ānanda piṇḍapātā samasamaphalā samavipākā ativiya aññehi piṇḍapātehi mahapphalatarā ca mahānisaṃsatarā ca, katame dve, yañca piṇḍapātaṃ paribhuñjitvā*

*tathāgato anuttaraṃ sammāsambodhiṃ abhisambujjhi; yañca piṇḍapātaṃ paribhuñjitvā tathāgato anupādisesāya nibbānadhātuyā parinibbāyati. (D. ii. 135)*

25. *Abyāvaṭā tumhe Ānanda hotha tathāgatassa sarīrapūjāyā'ti. (D. ii. 141)*

25. *Pūjetha naṃ pūjaniyassa dhātuṃ. Evaṃ kira saggamito gamissathā'ti. (Vv. 75 v 8)*

26. *Bhagavato gacchantassa ayaṃ acetanā mahāpathavī ninnaṃ unnamati, unnataṃ onamatī'ti. (cf. DA. 45)*

26. *Bhagavato pādo sakalikāya khato'ti. (Vin. ii. 193)*

27. *Āsavānaṃ khayā samaṇo hotī'ti. (A. ii. 238)*

27. *Catubbhi dhammehi samaṅgibhūtaṃ, taṃ ve naraṃ samaṇaṃ āhu loke'ti. Tatrime cattāro dhammā — khanti, appāhāratā, ratiippahānaṃ, ākiñcaññaṃ. (Ku. 5. p 204, Burmese Piṭaka)*

28. *Mamaṃ vā bhikkhave pare vaṇṇaṃ bhāseyyuṃ, dhammassa vā, saṅghassa vā vaṇṇaṃ bhāseyyuṃ, tatra tumhehi na Ānando, na somanassaṃ, na cetaso uppilāvitattaṃ karaṇīya'nti. (D. i. 3)*

28. *Rājāhamasmi selāti, dhammarājā anuttaro. Dhammena cakkaṃ vattemi, cakkaṃ appaṭivattiya'nti. (M. Sta92; Sn. v 554)*

29. *Ahiṃsāya cara loke, piyo hohisi mammivā'ti. (Jā. iv. 71 v 9)*

29. *Niggaṇhe niggahārahaṃ, paggaṇhe paggahāraha'nti. (Jā. v. 116)*

30. *Akkodhano vigatakhilohamasmī'ti. (Sn. v 19)*

31. *Etadaggaṃ bhikkhave mama sāvakānaṃ bhikkhūnaṃ iddhimantānaṃ yadidaṃ Mahāmoggallāno'ti. (A. i. 23)*

32. *Tathāgatappavedito bhikkhave dhammavinayo vivaṭo virocati no paṭicchanno'ti. (A. i. 283)*

32. *Pātimokkhudeso kevalañca vinayapiṭakaṃ pihitaṃ paṭicchannaṃ. (Vin. i. 115)*

33. *Sampajānamusāvāde pārājiko hotī'ti.* (*Vin.* *iii.* *94*)

33. *Sampajānamusāvāde lahukaṃ āpattiṃ āpajjati ekassa santike desanāvatthuka'nti.* (*Vin.* *iv.* *59*)

34. *Pubbeva bodhisattānaṃ mātāpitaro niyatā honti, bodhi niyatā hoti, aggasāvakā niyatā honti, putto niyato hoti, upaṭṭhāko niyato hotī'ti.* (*Mahāpadhāna Sutta.* *D.* *ii.* *11ff*)

34. *Tusite kāye ṭhito bodhisatto aṭṭha mahāvilokanāni viloketi; kālaṃ viloketi, dīpaṃ .. desaṃ .. kulaṃ .. janettiṃ .. āyuṃ .. māsaṃ .. nekkhammaṃ viloketī'ti.* (*Jā.* *i.* *48*)

35. *Na bhikkhave attānaṃ pātetabbaṃ, yo pāteyya, yathādhammo kāretabbo'ti.* (*Vin.* *iii.* *82*)

36. *Mettāya bhikkhave cetovimuttiyā āsevitāya bhāvitāya bahulīkatāya yānīkatāya vatthukatāya anuṭṭhitāya paricitāya susamāraddhāya ekādasānisaṃsā pāṭikaṅkhā. Katame ekādasa, sukhaṃ supati, sukhaṃ paṭibujjhati, na pāpakaṃ supinaṃ passati, manussānaṃ piyo hoti, amansussānaṃ piyo hoti, devatā rakkhanti, nāssa aggi vā visaṃ vā satthaṃ vā kamati, tuvaṭaṃ cittaṃ samādhiyati, mukhavaṇṇo vippasīdati, asammūḷho kālaṃ karoti, uttariṃ appaṭivijjhanto brahmalokūpago hotī'ti.* (*A.* *v.* *342*)

36. *Sāmo kumāro mettāvihārī migasaṅghena parivuto pavane vicaranto pīḷiyakkhena raññā viddho visapītena sallena tattheva mucchito patito'ti.* (*Jā.* *vi.* *76*)

38. *Mahosadhassa bhariyā amarā nāma itthī gāmake ṭhapitā pavutthapatikā raho nisinnā vivittā rājappaṭisamaṃ sāmikaṃ karitvā sahassena nimantīyamāna pāpaṃ nākāsi'ti.* (*Jā.* *vi.* *367*)

39. *Vigatabhayasantāsā arahanto'ti.* (*Dhp.* *v* *351;* *Sn.* *v* *621*)

39. *Nagare rājagahe dhanapālakaṃ hatthiṃ bhagavati opatantaṃ disvā pañca khīṇāsavasatāni pariccajitvā jinavaraṃ pakkantāni disāvidisaṃ ekaṃ ṭhapetvā theraṃ Ānandaṃ.* (*Vin.* *ii* *.194*)

40. *Tathāgatena Sāriputtamoggallānappamukhe bhikkhusaṅghe paṇāmite cātumeyyakā ca sakyā brahmā ca sahampati*

*bījūpamañca vacchataraṇūpamañca upadassetvā bhagavantaṃ pasādesuṃ khamāpesuṃ nijjhattaṃ akaṃsū'ti.* (M. Sta. 67)

41. *Santhavato bhayaṃ jātaṃ, niketā jāyate rajo. Aniketamasanthavaṃ, etaṃ ve munidassana'nti.* (Sn. v 207)

41. *Vihāre kāraye ramme, vāsayettha bahussute'ti.* (Vin. ii. 147; Sn. v 100)

42. *Uttiṭṭhe nappamajjeyya, udare saṃyato siyā'ti.* (Dhp. v 168)

42. *Ahaṃ kho panudāyi appekadā iminā pattena samatittikampi bhuñjāmi, tiyyopi bhuñjāmi'ti.* (M. ii. 7)

43. *Ahamasmi bhikkhave brāhmaṇo yācayogo sadā payatapāṇi antimadehadharo anuttaro bhisakko sallakatto'ti.* (Iti. 101)

43. *Etadaggaṃ bhikkhave mama sāvakānaṃ bhikkhūnaṃ appābādhānaṃ yadidaṃ bākulo'ti.* (A. i. 24)

44. *Tathāgato bhikkhave arahaṃ sammāsambuddho anuppannassa maggassa uppādethā'ti.* (S. iii. 66; S. i. 190)

44. *Addasaṃ khvāhaṃ bhikkhave purāṇaṃ maggaṃ purāṇaṃ añjasaṃ pubbakehi sammāsambuddhehi anuyāta'nti.* (S. ii. 105)

45. *Pubbe vāhaṃ manussabhūto samāno sattānaṃ aviheṭhakajātiko ahosi'nti.* (D. iii. 166)

45. *Lomasakassapo nāma isi samāno anekasate pāṇe ghātayitvā vājapeyyuṃ mahāyaññaṃ yajī'ti.* (Jā. iii. 514f)

46. *Vamissametanti parāmasanto, kāsāvamaddakkhi dhajaṃ isīnaṃ. Dukkhena phuṭṭhassudapādi saññā, arahaddhajo sabbhi avajjharūpo'ti.* (Jā. v. 49)

46. *Jotipālamāṇavo samāno kassapaṃ bhagavantaṃ arahantaṃ sammāsambuddhaṃ muṇḍakavādena samaṇakavādena asabbhāhi pharusāhi vācāhi akkosi paribhāsī.* (M. ii. 47)

47. *Ghaṭikārassa kumbhakārassa āvesanaṃ sabbaṃ temāsaṃ ākāsacchadanaṃ aṭṭhāsi, na devotivassī'ti.* (M. ii. 53)

47. *Kassapassa tatthāgatassa kuṭi ovassatī'ti.* (M. ii. 54)

49. *Gāthābhigītaṃ me abhojaneyyuṃ, sampassataṃ brāhmaṇa nesa dhammo. Gāthābhigītaṃ panudanti buddhā, dhamme satī brāhmaṇa vuttiresā'ti.* (S. i. 167; Sn. v 81)

50. *Tathāgatena catūhi ca asaṅkheyyehi kappānaṃ satasahassena ca etthantare sabbaññutañāṇaṃ paripācitaṃ mahato janakāyassa samuddharaṇāyā'ti.* (cf. Cp. i. 1)

50. *Appossukkatāya cittaṃ nami, no dhammadesanāyā'ti.* (Vin. i. 5; cf. S. i. 136)

51. *Na me ācariyo atthi, sadiso me na vijjati.* (Vin. i. 88; M. i. 171)

51. *Iti kho bhikkhave āḷāro kālāmo ācariyo me samāno antevāsiṃ maṃ samānaṃ attanā samasamaṃ ṭhapesi, uḷārāya ca maṃ pūjāya pūjesī'ti.* (M. i. 165)

52. *Aṭṭhānametaṃ bhikkhave anavakāso, yaṃ ekissā lokadhātuyā dve arahanto sammāsambuddhā apubbaṃ acarimaṃ uppajjeyyuṃ, netaṃ ṭhānaṃ vijjatī'ti.* (M. iii. 65; A. i. 27; Vbh. 336)

53. *Saṅghe Gotami dehi, saṅghe te dinne ahañceva pūjito bhavissāmi saṅgho cā'ti.* (M. iii. 253)

53. *Ekapuggalo bhikkhave loke uppajjamāno uppajjati bahujanahitāya bahujanasukhāya lokānukampāya atthāya hitāya sukhāya devamanussānaṃ katamo ekapuggalo, tathāgato arahaṃ sammāsambuddho.* (A. i. 21)

54. *Gihino vāhaṃ bhikkhave pabbajitassa vā sammāpaṭipattiṃ vaṇṇemi, gihī vā bhikkhave pabbajito vā sammāpaṭipanno sammāpaṭipattādhikaraṇahetu ārādhako hoti ñāyaṃ dhammaṃ kusala'nti.* (M. ii. 197; A. i. 69 § 10)

55. *Na kho panāhaṃ imāya kaṭukāya dukkarakārikāya adhigacchāmi uttarimanussadhammaṃ alamariyañāṇadassanavisesaṃ, siyā nu kho añño maggo bodhāyā'ti.* (M. i. 246)

55. *Ārambhatha nikkhamatha, yuñjatha buddhasāsane. Dhunātha maccuno senaṃ, naḷāgāraṃva kuñjaro'ti.* (S. i. 156; Kvu. 203)

57. *Arahā ekaṃ vedanaṃ vedayati kāyikaṃ na cetasika'nti.* (Untraced)

58. *Jānantassa kukkuccaṃ hoti, kukkucce sati āvaraṇaṃ hoti, āvaṭe citte dhammābhisamayo na hotī'ti.* (Untraced)

59. *Yo sīlavā dussīlesu dadāti dānaṃ, dhammena laddhaṃ supasannacitto. Abhisaddahaṃ kammaphalaṃ uḷāraṃ, sā dakkhiṇā dāyakato visujjhatī'ti.* (M. Sta. 142)

61. *Nippapañcārāmā bhikkhave viharatha nippapañcaratino'ti.* (Untraced but cf. M. i. 65)

62. *Yo gihī arahattaṃ patto, dve vāssa gatiyo bhavanti anaññā, tasmiṃ yeva divase pabbajati vā parinibbāyati vā. No so divaso sakkā atikkametu'nti.* (Untraced)

63. *Vigatasatisammosā kho mahārāja arahanto, natthi arahantānaṃ satisammosoti.* (Untraced. cf. Pts.Contr. 114)

64.— *katamāni tīṇi, sacetanā vā acetanā vā ajarāmarā loke natthi, saṅkhārānaṃ niccatā natthi, paramatthena sattūpaladdhi natthi.* (Untraced)

65. *Ākāso mahārāja, akammajo ahetujo anutujo, nibbānaṃ mahārāja akammajaṃ ahetujaṃ anutujaṃ. Ime kho mahārāja, dve akammajā ahetujā anutujā'ti.* (Miln. 268.)

69. *Sūriyassapi tāva tejosampannassa rogo uppajjissati, kimaṅgaṃ pana aññesaṃ satthānaṃ, natthi bhante esā vibhatti aññassa aññatra tavādisena buddhimatā'ti.* (Miln. 274.)

72. Twenty-five Conditions Causing Weakness

*Kodha, apanāho, makkho, paḷāso, issā, macchariyaṃ, māyā, sāṭheyyuṃ, tambho, sārambho, māno, atimāno, mado, pamādo, thinamiddhaṃ, tandi (nandī), ālasyaṃ, pāpamittatā, rūpā, saddā, gandhā, rasā, phoṭṭhabbā, khudāpipāsā, arati* ... (Miln. 289.)

81. *Nibbānaṃ na atītaṃ, na anāgataṃ, na paccuppannaṃ, na uppannaṃ, na anuppannaṃ na uppādanīya'nti.* (Untraced)

81. *So appavattatthāya maggaṃ āyūhati gavesati bhāveti bahulīkaroti tassa tadatthaṃ sati santiṭṭhati, tadatthaṃ vīriyaṃ*

*santiṭṭhati, tadatthaṃ pīti santiṭṭhati, tassa taṃ cittaṃ aparāparaṃ manasīkaroto pavattaṃ samatikkamitvā appavattaṃ okkamati, appavattamanuppatc mahārāja sammāpaṭipanno 'nibbānaṃ sacchikarotī'ti vuccati.* (Miln. 326)

## A Question Solved by Inference

*Na pupphagandho paṭivātameti, na candanaṃ taggaramallikā vā. Satañca gandho paṭivātameti, sabbā disā sappuriso pavāyati.* (Dhp. v 54)

*Amataṃ te bhikkhave paribhuñjanti, ye kāyagatāsatiṃ paribhunjantī'ti.* (A. i. 45)

## The Ascetic Practices

*Suddhājīvaṃ sukhaphalaṃ anavajjaṃ na paradukkhāpanaṃ abhayaṃ asampīḷanaṃ ekantavaḍḍikaṃ aparihāniyaṃ amāyaṃ ārakkhā patthitadadaṃ sabbasattadamanaṃ saṃvarahitaṃ patirūpaṃ anissitaṃ vippamuttaṃ rāgakkhayaṃ dosakkhayaṃ mohakkhayaṃ mānappahānaṃ kuvitakkacchedanaṃ kaṅkhavitaraṇaṃ kossajjaviddhaṃsanaṃ aratippahānaṃ khamanaṃ atulaṃ appamānaṃ sabbadukkhakkhayagamanaṃ.* (Miln. 351)

## Simile

60. *Sassataṃ ucchedaṃ taṃ jīvaṃ taṃ sarīraṃ aññaṃ jīvaṃ aññaṃ sarīraṃ taduttamaṃ aññaduttamaṃ akaṭamabhabbaṃ apurisakāraṃ abrāhmacariyavāsaṃ sattavināsaṃ navasattapātibhāvaṃ saṅkhārasassatabhavaṃ yo karoti so paṭisaṃvedeti añño karoti añño paṭisaṃvedeti kammaphaladassanā ca kiriyaphaladiṭṭhi ca ito evarūpāni ceva aññāni ca vivādapathāni apanetvā saṅkhārānaṃ sabhāvaṃ paramasuññataṃ nirīhanijjīvataṃ (nisattanijīvataṃ) accantaṃ suññataṃ ādiyitabbaṃ.* (Miln. 413)

61. *Yadūnakaṃ taṃ saṇati, yaṃ pūraṃ santameva taṃ. Aḍḍakumbhūpamo [rittakumbhūpamo] bālo, rahado pūro'va paṇḍito'ti.* (Sn. v 721)

# Bibliography


## Translations of the Milinda Pañha

Horner, I.B., – translator.
*Milinda's Questions,* 2 Vols. Reprint, London, 1969.

Rhys Davids, T.W., – translator.
*The Questions of King Milinda,* Vol. XXXV. and XXXVI. Sacred Books of the East, Oxford 1890, 1894 respectively. Reprints: New York, 1973, Delhi, 1969.

## Pali Texts of the Milinda Pañha

Burmese script, Chaṭṭha Saṅgīti Edition. Rangoon 1960.

Trenckner, V., – editor.
Roman script edition, London, 1880. Reprint, London 1962.

Jaini, Padmanabh S. – editor.
*Milinda Ṭika,* roman script edition, London 1961.

## Secondary Sources

Bhikkhu Thich Minh Chau M.A. PhD. – author.
*Milinda Pañha and Nāgasenabhikshusūtra, (A Comparative Study)* Sole Agent: Firma K.L.M., Calcutta

Quintos, L. (R.C.) – author.
*Buddhism in Dialogue (The Moral System of Buddhism According to the Milinda Pañha with a Christian Theological Reflection)* Cardinal BEA Institute, Loyola School of Theology, Atteneo de Manilla University, 1977.

Rabindra Nath Basu M.A. PhD. – author.
*A Critical Study of the Milinda Pañha,* Firma K.L.M. Ltd, Calcutta, 1978.

Rhys Davids, Mrs. C.A.F – author.
*The Milinda Questions (An Inquiry into its Place in the History of Buddhism with a Theory as to its Author),* London, 1930.

## Historical Sources

Smith, V.A. – author.
*ASOKA – The Buddhist Emperor of India,* Clarendon Press, Oxford, 1901.
*Early History of India (Including Alexander's Campaigns),* Clarendon Press, Oxford, 1924.

Rhys Davids, T.W. – author.
*BUDDHISM – Its History and Literature,* London, 1896. Reprint, Calcutta, 1962.
*Buddhist India,* Calcutta, 1950. Delhi, 1971.

Law, B.C. – author.
*A History of Pali Literature,* Vol II, 1933, pp.353-372.
*Geography of Early Buddhism*

Narain, A.K. – author.
*The Indo Greeks,* Oxford, 1957.

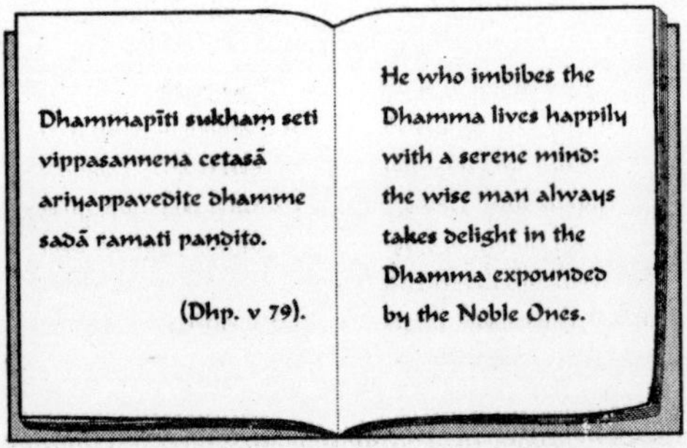
Dhammapīti sukhaṃ seti
vippasannena cetasā
ariyappavedite dhamme
sadā ramati paṇḍito.
(Dhp. v 79).
He who imbibes the
Dhamma lives happily
with a serene mind:
the wise man always
takes delight in the
Dhamma expounded
by the Noble Ones.

# Index



## A

of Great Benefit 59
Offences of, 78
*Arahantship* 1, 77
Fruit of, 95
Only Attained by Zealousness 98
Qualities Needed for, 100
Ascetic Practices *(dhutaṅga)* xx, 2, 64, 71, 97, 99, 109
28 Virtues of, 121
Ascetics and Brahmans 42
Asoka xviii
Death of, xix
Inscriptions of, xviii
Missions Sent by, xviii
Asoka Park 1
Assagutta 1
Asseveration of Truth 39
Attachment *(upādāna)* 13, 21, 25
as Causal Link 15, 16
Attention *(manasikāra)* 17
Austerities *(dukkarakārikā)* 109
Practice of, 72, 83
Author of *Milinda Pañha* xx
Aversion *(paṭigha)* 12

# B

Bactria xvi, xviii, xix
*Bhikkhus* from, xix
Founding of, xviii
New rulers of, xix
Rise of, xix
Bactrian Greeks *(yonaka)* 2, 109
Became Buddhists xvi
Bakkula, the Healthiest *Bhikkhu* 64
Bases of Success *(iddhipāda)* 7, 9, 43, 93, 95
Becoming *(bhava)* 21
as Causal Link 15, 16
Being *(satta)* 14
Transmigration of, 23
Best of Men 64
Bindusāra xviii
Birth *(jāti)* 21
as Causal Link 15, 16
Birth, Old Age, Disease and Death
Anxiety Arising from, 91
Deliverance from, 63, 95
Destruction of, 59
Bodhi Tree 26, 42, 110
Bodhisatta 110
as Elephant 66
as Lomassa Kassapa 65
as Vessantara 38, 82
Austerities of, 72, 83
Compared to Devadatta 60
Prolonged Practice of, 68
Teachers of, 69
Weakness of, 65
Body *(rūpa khandha)* 3
Bones 31
Brahmā 110
Disciple of the Buddha 26
Realm of, 29, 30, 31, 60, 66, 109
Requests Buddha to Teach 69
Brahmā Sahampati 62
Brahman 110
Buddha as, 64
Brahman Sela 52, 55
Buddha
18 Characteristics of, 37
Arising of Two Together 70
as *Brahmacārin* 26
Boasting of, 55
Compassion of, 37, 51
Discoverer of the Path 65
Equanimity of, 43
Existence of, 22, 24, 93
Honours Paid to, 34
Incomparable 22
Kassapa 66
Last Meal of, 53
Modesty of, 51
Omniscience of, 25, 36, 80
One Who Sheds Blood of, 89
Ordination of, 26
Perfect Speech of, 45, 52
Perfection of, 42
Possessiveness of, 48
Purity of, 41
Reluctance of, 68

Thinking about, 28
Unlike His Parents 26
Buddhaghosa
Editor of *Milinda Pañha* xvi
Buddha's Change of Heart 62
Buddha's Foot is Injured 54
Buddha's Teachers 69

C

Cūḷapanthaka 52
Cause *(hetu)* 11, 80
Causes of Earthquakes 108
Celibate *(Brahmacārin)* 26, 110
Chandragupta xviii
Clarification *(sampasādana)* 8
Clear Insight *(adhigama)* 41
Coins of Menander xv
Compassion *(karuṇā)*
Meditation on, 94
Conceiving *(cetayita)* 18
Concentration *(samādhi)* 7, 8, 10, 95, 96, 100, 109, 111
Characteristic of, 9
Hindrances to, 108
of the Buddha 35, 64
Conception
Dilemma of, 40
Condition *(paccaya)* 11
Conduct *(cāra)* 41, 110
Confidence *(saddhā)* 7, 42
Characteristic of, 8
Lack of, 47
Consciousness *(viññāṇa)*
Aggregate of, 3
as Causal Link 15
Characteristic of, 18, 32
Contact *(phasso)* 15, 17
as Causal Link 15, 16
Characteristic of, 17
Distinguishing of, 32
Controlling Faculties *(indriya)* 9, 93, 95
Corpses
as Meditation Objects, 94
Craving *(taṇhā)* 15, 21, 79, 90, 92, 94
as Causal Link 15, 16

D

Danger *(ādīṇava)* 94
Death *(maraṇaṃ)* 15, 16, 21
Army of, 72
Fear of, 45
of Asoka xix
of Menander xv
Premature, 87
Protection from, 46
Rebirth after, 6
Defilements *(kilesa)* 7, 55, 56, 67, 72, 73
Antidote to, 95
as Cause of Rebirth 6
as Obstruction to *Paritta* 47
Bondage of, 62
Destruction of, 10
Reflection on, 96
Deity *(deva)* 53, 88, 107, 108
Delusion *(moha)* 33
Demerit *(apuñña)* 3, 30
of Killing Living Beings 48
Power of, 47
Demetrius xvi
Demons *(yakkha)* 80
Desire, Hatred and Delusion *(rāga, dosa, moha)* 33, 89
Destruction of, 97
Fire of, 91
Freedom from, 94, 95
Heat of, 35
Removal of, 42
Those Full of, 36
Desirelessness *(appaṇihita)*
Attainment of, 95
Despair *(upāyāsa)* 15, 16, 21, 87, 92, 95
Devadatta
Causes a Schism 49
Ordination of, 37
Prosperity of, 60
Rock Thrown by, 41, 54
Swallowed by the Earth 35

# H



# I



# J



# K

## N



## O



## P

# T

## U



## V



## W